"At the end of the day, leading transformational change is all about driving and sustaining great business results with and through other people. *The Secret Sauce for Leading Transformational Change* offers multiple perspectives on how to make it happen in highly pragmatic ways."

Chris Kastner, *President and CEO, Huntington Ingalls Industries*

"Leaders and organizations must master transformational change to remain relevant and viable. *The Secret Sauce* is a powerful resource for practical insights into the what, why, and how."

Professor Edward E. Lawler III, *Director, USC Marshall School of Business Center for Effective Organizations*

"Now more than ever, businesspeople are looking for durable and practical methods to lead through transformational change, and *The Secret Sauce* provides both. It provides the 'what' and 'so what' for transformational change in a manner that is both thought-provoking and immediately applicable."

Peter Mulford, *Executive Vice President and Chief Innovation Officer, BTS Inc.*

"The demand for transformational change has never been greater, and the practical guidance offered in *The Secret Sauce for Leading Transformational Change* is top flight. Highly recommended for CEOs, board members, and senior leaders as we address this demand."

Jane Edison Stevenson, *Vice-Chair, Board and CEO Services, Korn Ferry*

"Ian's lifetime of experiences has generated a marvelous compendium of ideas with impact. Transformation happens when thoughtful colleagues share insights on truth, talent, timing, and tools."

Dave Ulrich, *Rensis Likert Professor Ross School of Business, University of Michigan; Partner, The RBL Group*

The Secret Sauce for Leading Transformational Change

Written by a collaborative, diverse, and inclusive community of contributors and business experts, this book is about leading transformational change on an individual, team, organizational, and societal level.

Most large-scale transformational change happens because of unanticipated, unaddressed, unplanned disruptions which raise questions about what it takes to lead, survive, and even thrive in periods of transformational change. This book answers these critical questions:

1. What do leaders who drive and sustain successful transformational change actually do?
2. Why do we so often fail to lead and sustain transformational change?
3. All transformation is change, but is all change transformational?

This first-of-its-kind book offers a variety of lenses and perspectives, in the form of interviews, essays, and survey responses, with insights from business leaders, HR leaders, coaches, consultants, academics, thought leaders, and other transformational change experts.

The compilation of practical tools provides readers with a deep and diverse analysis of top-notch thinking and practices for leading transformational change. This work is fundamental to aspiring leaders, professionals, and academics who wish to learn the secret sauce for leading transformational change.

Ian Ziskin, President, EXec EXcel Group LLC, has 40 years of experience as a business leader, board advisor and member, coach, consultant, entrepreneur, teacher, speaker, and author. He is the Co-Founder and Partner of Business inSITE Group (BiG), Co-Founder of the Consortium for Change (C4C), and Co-Founder of the CHREATE Project. His global leadership experience includes Chief Human Resources Officer and/or other senior leadership roles with three Fortune 100 companies – Northrop Grumman, Qwest Communications, and TRW. He has a Master of Industrial and Labor Relations degree from Cornell University and is a magna cum laude graduate of Binghamton University with a Bachelor of Science degree in Management. Ian has written dozens of articles, blogs, and book chapters on the future of work, HR, leadership, coaching, and HR's role with the board of directors.

The Secret Sauce for Leading Transformational Change

Ian Ziskin
and
The Consortium for Change (C4C)

Foreword By
Dr. Ronald D. Sugar
Chairman Emeritus, Northrop Grumman Corporation
Board Director, Amgen, Apple, Chevron, and Uber

 Routledge
Taylor & Francis Group

NEW YORK AND LONDON

Cover image: George Bloomfield

First published 2022
by Routledge
605 Third Avenue, New York, NY 10158

and by Routledge
4 Park Square, Milton Park, Abingdon, Oxon, OX14 4RN

Routledge is an imprint of the Taylor & Francis Group, an informa business

© 2022 Ian Ziskin

Library of Congress Cataloging-in-Publication Data
A catalog record for this book has been requested

ISBN: 978-1-032-12985-3 (hbk)
ISBN: 978-1-032-12988-4 (pbk)
ISBN: 978-1-003-22713-7 (ebk)

DOI: 10.4324/9781003227137

Typeset in Adobe Caslon Pro
by Apex CoVantage, LLC

For my granddaughter, Zoe, and for her little sister who will be born right about the time this book is published, because they represent why leading transformational change matters.

Contents

Foreword – Truth, Talent, and Timing

By Dr. Ronald D. Sugar

Over my five-decade career as an engineer, CFO, CEO, and board director, I have led or participated in more than a few transformational changes. I have learned a lot about what works and does not work, sometimes the hard way. But, one learning stands out for sure: leading transformational change is a team sport.

Ian Ziskin, the lead author of this important new book, and I first worked together 25 years ago. He served as my chief HR officer twice – first at TRW Inc. then at Northrop Grumman Corporation. Together, we learned that leading transformational change is a product of defining a clear purpose, understanding what to change, knowing what to preserve, and building collective energy among the people who needed to embrace the hard work to make it happen.

I have been around businesses and leaders in trouble, or growing, or performing well, or needing to change – sometimes several of these at once. In every case, three things seem to have made the biggest difference in leading successful transformational change: Truth, Talent, and Timing.

Truth

No person or organization can change unless and until they first confront reality. When I was Chairman and CEO of Northrop Grumman, we had an operating philosophy, "In this company, we want good news to travel up the line fast, but bad news to travel even faster." That meant we wanted to know what was working well in the organization, what was not, and to know soon enough to do something about it.

Situational awareness of what is happening around us is a crucial ingredient for leading transformational change. You cannot fix things you cannot see or refuse to acknowledge. Try not to allow your hopes or biases to cloud your judgment about what is really going on around you. Face the truth, and deal with it.

Talent

Surround yourself with the very best people, and listen to and learn from them. They will help you understand what is working and what is not. I really embrace the saying, "In this room, all of us together are smarter than any of us alone."

As a business leader and board member, I have always valued having around me a few "free electrons," people who think differently, have unique perspectives and capabilities, and are willing to challenge conventional wisdom. Highly talented people with diverse perspectives make a world of difference in leading transformational change. Give your free electrons the platform and voice to help you see the need for and drive change.

Timing

Very few leaders have ever said to me, "I wish I had waited longer to make that big change." In retrospect, they realized they should have moved more quickly and decisively. There is always a desire to get more data, to buy more time, and to try not to make a big mistake. But at some point, you need to make the call, and often failing to take action timely will create a worse outcome. Trust your gut. It is your own personal AI algorithm trained by experiences over your lifetime.

> *A final thought: To me, Truth, Talent, and Timing are absolutely necessary ingredients for success. But they, by themselves, are not sufficient. Transformation is not simply an analytic or intellectual exercise. It is a deeply emotional and often wrenching experience that can span a wide arc in space and time. So before you embark, you as the leader need to look inside yourself, fully buy in personally, and then commit to doing.*

Dr. Ronald D. Sugar *is Chairman Emeritus of Northrop Grumman and served as the company's Chairman and CEO from 2003 to 2009. He is a member of the Boards of Directors of Amgen, Apple, Chevron, and Uber.*

Part I

Context

Introduction – The Spirit of Abundance

The idea for this book began during the COVID-19 pandemic of 2020–2022 with my thoughts about the transformational changes taking place in people's personal and work lives, and society at large. Over 935,000 people died in the United States, with a total of nearly 6,000,000 lives lost globally as of this writing. This unprecedented two-year period, with reverberations expected for years to come, was characterized by massive disruptions including economic instability, racial and social injustice, declines in mental and physical well-being, remote school and work challenges, and political divisions. We have all been living with change and uncertainty, followed by more uncertainty and more change.

These monumental changes, exacerbated by lockdown fever, prompted me to think about what it takes to lead, survive, and even thrive in periods of transformational change. They also made me want to write this book in a highly collaborative, community-minded way. I became strongly motivated to work with colleagues, friends, and experts who represent diverse thinking and perspectives, and who could help examine transformational change through a wide range of lenses. To be honest, I also needed human connection, and to do something fun. These were things the pandemic had stolen from us all for more than 24 months.

The core group for this collaborative book project began with the Consortium for Change (C4C), a community network of independent coaches, consultants, and transformational change experts I co-founded in 2018 with one of my business partners, Lacey Leone McLaughlin. C4C is based on *The Spirit of Abundance*, a shorthand way of saying that our purpose is to share business opportunities, competitive intelligence, learning and ideas, and best practices that allow us to collaborate on behalf of clients, rather than to compete among ourselves. We encourage, support, and raise the bar for one another. We believe we are stronger together than alone. As a result, our clients win, and so do we.

DOI: 10.4324/9781003227137-2

C4C Guiding Principles

1. Abundance – We collaborate within, so everyone can win
2. Surge Capacity – We deliver more capability for clients together than alone
3. Business Referrals – We share opportunities and fees to provide clients with trusted alternatives
4. Inclusion – We represent depth and breadth of backgrounds, experiences, perspectives, geographics, industries, and diversity in all dimensions
5. Reciprocity – We network, share best practices, teach, learn, respect one another's time, and get what we give
6. Agility – We act and respond quickly and operate with a light, non-bureaucratic, entrepreneurial, and voluntary touch

(For information on C4C and our members, visit https://businessinsitegroup. com/consortium-for-change/).

Ultimately, 25 C4C members contributed to this book (not including me), those with particular interest and expertise in leading transformational change. These peers have big ideas and passion related to transformational change. Before we get too far into the book, I want to acknowledge the commitment and collaboration of my C4C colleagues who have contributed their expertise to *The Secret Sauce for Leading Transformational Change*:

Kelly Bean	Lori Heffelfinger	Cheryl Perkins
Dr. John Boudreau	Jake Jacobs	Patrick R. Powaser, Ph.D.
Dr. Beth Banks Cohn	Karen Jaw-Madson	Susan Robertson
Rebecca Feder	Sophia Kristjansson	Deb Seidman
Steve Fitzgerald	Dr. Orly Maravankin	Adrienne Shoch
Maria Forbes	Kim McEachron	Tracy Tyler
Barbara Frankel	Jennifer E. McEwen, Ph.D.	David Yudis, Psy.D., MBA
Jennifer Green	Lacey Leone McLaughlin	
Marisa Harris	Linda Naiman	

Our C4C core group was only the beginning of our collaboration strategy. We then included the practical experience and perspectives of an additional several hundred leaders and thinkers who contributed to our book through essays, interviews, a survey, and tools, all focused on the art and science of leading transformational change. The book is truly a product of collective wisdom, shaped by stories of success, failure, elation, and frustration. As we will argue in the book, transformational change takes a village, and it is not always easy, pretty, or successful.

We have chosen to include diverse and sometimes conflicting perspectives on transformational change, taking advantage of insights and experiences shared by CEOs and other senior business leaders, CHROs and other senior

HR leaders, transformational change experts, authors, coaches, consultants, and many more. Their stories and insights address large-scale transformational change affecting individuals, teams, and organizations, and also suggest implications for society at large.

As a reader, you can expect the following from *The Secret Sauce for Leading Transformational Change*:

- Broad and diverse perspectives from a wide range of leaders and other experts who have actually executed and delivered on transformational change, not just studied or written about it
- Vivid stories and lessons learned from real business and life situations
- Practical points of view and insights on what to do and how to do it, what not to do and why, as well as who is responsible for delivering and sustaining transformational change
- Useable tools, frameworks, and other resources that supplement our book content
- Confidence and inspiration to lead transformational change in your own organization and life

In addition, you will learn how to:

- Prioritize and sequence actions to lead transformational change
- Avoid common pitfalls, overcome obstacles, and minimize the risk of failure
- Determine whether change and transformation are the same or different
- Define "from what to what?" before beginning or leading any transformational change journey

The rich content and lessons learned included in our book are further supplemented by a companion website, www.transformationalchangebook.com, which provides additional insights on leading transformational change, the backgrounds of our contributing authors, and access to links for ordering the book as well as for scheduling related presentations and other speaking engagements.

The Spirit of Abundance has been an important guidepost in writing this book. We have done our best to create a diverse and inclusive community of book contributors, share insights about leading transformational change, and raise the bar for all those who wish to be better at understanding, leading, and executing successful and lasting transformational change.

We hope you find value in this book and ask that you share what you learn with others, in *The Spirit of Abundance*.

Ian Ziskin
Sag Harbor, New York
February 22, 2022

Chapter 1

From What to What?

1969 was a pivotal year in my life. As a kid growing up in the suburbs of Long Island, New York, it was the season the Knicks, Jets, and Mets all won championships in their respective professional sports of basketball, football, and baseball. For an 11-year-old who loved sports, everything seemed pretty awesome. Life was good, until it wasn't.

That year was also when my father, Ted Ziskin, began bumping into walls and other previously navigable objects. My mother, Marilyn, was the first to notice it. My brother Adam, age 7, and I were too busy being kids and doing our own things to pay attention to what was going on around us. We were oblivious, until we weren't.

Many, many months passed with seemingly endless doctor visits and a variety of hypotheses. Then, finally, a diagnosis. Multiple sclerosis.

My father's condition worsened over a two-year period. He was in and out of hospitals and nursing homes, able to come home on occasion but not for long. Loss of motor functions. Loss of bodily functions. Loss of dignity and independence for him, and a loss of normalcy and stability for our family. Finally, on June 5, 1971, loss of life. My father passed away in the hospital from complications related to his multiple sclerosis, ten days short of his 47th birthday.

It took me a week before I could cry and even longer to begin processing and understanding what had happened, let alone what was about to happen. After all, I was only 13 and my brother was only 9.

Our dad was a big dude, 6'3" tall and 260 pounds. His heart was bigger, and everyone knew him to be very helpful, generous, and hard-working. They called him Teddy, and the name fit, he was like a teddy bear. But, he also had high standards, big dreams, and a strong sense of right and wrong. If we lied or cut corners, we were not going to get away with it.

I have a few vivid memories of getting myself in trouble, but many more very fond memories of my dad buying all my friends ice cream from the ice cream truck or taking me for a chocolate egg cream (a New York drink made of milk, carbonated water, and flavored syrup). Ironically, egg creams contain neither eggs nor cream – and therefore, like so many things in life, they are not

DOI: 10.4324/9781003227137-3

all they appear to be. I will never forget the feel of his scratchy beard when he kissed me goodnight in bed, after returning home late from a long day at work.

My father loved my mother, his sons, his extended family and friends, and food. He could eat an entire pint of pistachio ice cream in one sitting, right out of the container. Yes, there is an ice cream theme going on here (my favorite is cookies and cream). I am a lot like my father and share his love of food. Stay tuned for an analysis of how pizza relates to leading transformational change in Chapter 10 of the book.

But, there is also another theme that began taking shape in my life over 50 years ago, starting with my father's illness and untimely death. Recognizing and facing transformational change.

Like the story about my father, transformational change can seem gradual, yet sudden, devastating, yet eye-opening. It can be seen as a challenge to overcome or an opportunity to seize. Leading transformational change can be a burden or a privilege. It can bring misery and pain or joy and strength. Transformational change can be the test or the proof.

My life changed forever between 1969 and 1971, but I had big decisions to make. Would I allow my father's death to define me, and if so, how? Would I be a victim and feel sorry for myself, and use this tragedy as an excuse? Or, would I confront reality, get focused, be resilient, grow up fast, and be better for living through the experience? Would I turn a negative into a positive?

These are the questions I like to think I asked myself back then when I was 13. More likely, I was probably just trying to figure out how to survive, make it through to the other side, and not give my mother or brother anything else to worry about. Fortunately, my mother and brother were very supportive of me, and we all looked out for one another. We turned out sane and strong, and I choose to believe my father would be very proud of us.

This pivotal time taught me many valuable life lessons. One such lesson has proven to be transformational for me, not only in life but in leadership. It is the importance of understanding and articulating, "from what to what?" This question is about knowing where you came from and where you are going. It implies knowing what is important and what is not, how you are going to get from point A to point B, and what you are going to change and preserve. Most importantly, it is the central question in leading transformational change.

As I write this book, supported by the contributions of so many knowledgeable and passionate transformational change experts, I cannot help but be reminded that 2021 was the 50th anniversary of my father's passing. Over the years, I have not spent much time feeling sorry for myself about his loss, although I do sometimes wonder how my life (as well as my family's and his) would be different had he lived much longer. Mostly, I have just tried to be the kind of person my father would have wanted and expected me to be.

Have I been successful? I will never really know. But, that has not stopped me from trying, every day. And, it has not prevented me from learning, growing, and changing. After all, transformational change starts with the individual, in this case, me.

The Secret Sauce for Leading Transformational Change is about leading transformational change on an individual, team, and organizational level – and it suggests some societal implications as well. Fundamentally, we wrote the book to answer the following critical questions:

1. What do leaders who drive and sustain successful transformational change actually do?
2. Why do we so often fail to lead and sustain transformational change?
3. Is it true that all transformation is change, but not all change is transformational?
4. From what to what?

In my experience, many of us perpetuate a myth about change – that successful transformational change is anticipated, planned for in advance, and well-executed ahead of the need. This perspective about leading transformational change seems enlightened, thoughtful, and therefore strategic. But, it is largely inaccurate.

Most large-scale transformational change comes about as a result of unanticipated, unaddressed, unplanned disruptions which in turn result in some kind of reaction or response. As heavyweight boxer Mike Tyson said to a reporter in advance of one of his bouts, "Everyone has a plan until they get punched in the mouth." Individuals, teams, organizations, and societies often get punched in the mouth. Then, they respond – some more effectively, intelligently, rationally, and urgently than others.

Are there many examples of well-conceived change initiatives and actions that were planned ahead of the curve? Of course, and we explore many such scenarios in this book. However, there are even more examples of people and organizations that lack situational awareness. They live in a perpetual state of denial, where key players do not see or want to see the need for transformational change, nor the ramifications of failing to act. We examine many of these situations in the book as well.

We address leading transformational change through a variety of lenses and perspectives, with insights from several hundred business leaders, HR leaders, coaches, consultants, academics, thought leaders, and other transformational change experts. We use essays, interviews, survey responses, and a compilation of practical tools to provide the reader with a deep and diverse analysis of top-notch thinking and practices for leading transformational change.

Our analysis begs the question, is transformational change typically driven by a specific need, or is it simply inevitable? I have always been fascinated by lyrics from the Bon Jovi song, "The More Things Change." "*The more things change, the more they stay the same.*" For purposes of this book, I propose a new way of thinking . . . "*The more things stay the same, the more they need to change.*" Individuals, teams, organizations, and societies seem to prefer stasis. Progress and prosperity often demand transformational change. Therein lurks the conflict, and limitless opportunities.

The Secret Sauce for Leading Transformational Change is organized into three distinct but integrated parts. The book provides Context, Insights, and Actions that combine to raise important questions, and provide essential answers, about leading transformational change.

Part I (Context), the Introduction and Chapters 1–2, includes this chapter and summarizes my inspiration and motivations for writing this book. It also includes an outline of how the book is organized, as well as an analysis of the top seven competing priorities that must be reconciled when effectively leading transformational change. This set of paradoxes previews change challenges expressed in different ways throughout the entire book.

Part II (Insights), Chapters 3–7, features three separate but interconnected sections. The first section, Expert Perspectives (Essays), Chapters 3, 4, and 5, presents 25 essays written by business, HR, and transformation leaders, as well as by coaches, consultants, academics, thought leaders, and others with expertise and experience in leading transformational change. These experts share their insights, perspectives, philosophies, and wisdom in a way that showcases a rich tapestry of ideas from which the reader can extract practical advice and creative inspiration. The essays are grouped according to whether their primary focus addresses Individual, Team, or Organizational aspects of transformational change. Each essay concludes with three things the contributors want you to know or do about successfully leading transformational change. The concepts and insights in each essay are different, but the pattern of recommendations and cautions is clear and compelling.

The second section, Leadership Storytelling (Interviews), Chapter 6, features interviews with eight CEOs and other senior business leaders who have driven significant transformational change efforts in very unique, complex organizations. The "from what to what?" associated with each story is different. Yet, the successes, failures, joys, frustrations, and lessons learned form a remarkably consistent pattern. And, as important as "leaders" are in leading transformational change, it becomes increasingly clear as our storytellers reveal their circumstances, that no one leads successful transformational change alone. As with the essays, all the leadership stories conclude with three things you should know or do about transformational change.

The third section, Crowdsourcing (Survey), Chapter 7, captures input from several hundred leaders and practitioners in response to one pivotal question, "*What is the single most important action or step a leader or organization can take to ensure successful and lasting transformational change?*" We identify three important themes for leading transformational change, as well as for minimizing the risk of crashing and burning along the way, supported by a sampling of survey responses that reinforce these common themes.

Part III of the book (Actions), Chapters 8–10, connects the dots among key lessons learned and emerging trends as suggested by the essays, interviews, survey findings, and other insights in prior book sections. These themes will help you clearly understand what successful and failed transformational change efforts look and feel like. They will also help you see around corners to anticipate where the practice of leading transformational change is heading, so you can be ready for and more aligned with the evolving body of knowledge and capability requirements. This part of the book highlights some key things you should not do, reveals the secret sauce for leading transformational change that simmers throughout each previous chapter, and addresses the question that every leader insists be answered: "What the f*#k does pizza have to do with leading transformational change?"

Our Appendix curates some of our favorite frameworks used by a handful of our contributing transformational change experts. These select tools provide practical roadmaps for tackling the toughest transformational change challenges.

The book presents independent, diverse, and sometimes divergent views on leading transformational change, while simultaneously trumpeting a highly integrated and remarkably consistent set of concepts and actionable ideas. Most notably, a formula for successfully leading transformational change emerges in stark relief as the book unfolds. There really *is* a secret sauce for leading transformational change!

Chapter 2

The Beauty of "And"

Leading transformational change, perhaps more than any other aspect of leadership, is highly dependent on the will and skill to reconcile competing priorities. It often comes down to balancing incongruous interests and to mastering paradox. But, truly effective transformational change is not about winners and losers, or either/or. It is about the beauty of "*and*."

My experience, further reinforced by the findings and perspectives in this book, has taught me that leading transformational change demands embracing the notion that two contradictory things can be true at the same time. There are seven paradoxes that matter most in leading transformational change:

1. Past *and* Future
2. Reality *and* Aspiration
3. Facts *and* Feelings
4. Speed *and* Rhythm
5. Flexibility *and* Focus
6. Difference *and* Improvement
7. Change *and* Transformation

Past *and* Future

Chapter 1 is titled, "From What to What?" for a reason. It is intended to introduce early in the book an unavoidable tension associated with transformational change. Most of us are faced with the same question no matter what circumstances we are confronting, "What are we going to preserve about our past, while simultaneously changing things to create a new and improved future?"

Transformational change is clearly about doing things differently, better, smarter, cheaper, and faster; or more creatively, sustainably, and safely; or less annoyingly, selfishly, and stupidly. It implies endless permutations about how individuals, teams, organizations, or societies can be enhanced to promote efficiency or effectiveness, as well as to maximize harmony or happiness. But, it is not all about the future – how the "world will be a better place when . . ." Transformational change is also about the past.

DOI: 10.4324/9781003227137-4

Leading transformational change is a legitimate place for thoughtful examination of what has worked well, what got us here, and what we should not mess up in the face of other changes that must take hold. The past includes strengths that must be preserved and serves as the basis upon which the future is defined and refined. Transformational change is not about blowing everything up and starting over, although that imagery is often invoked. Instead, it is about creating and outlining an effective balance between respecting the past *and* falling in love with the future.

Reality *and* Aspiration

Many individuals, teams, organizations, and societies have some kind of vision, mission, values, behaviors, or principles to which they aspire. These rules of the road set the tone for shared expectations and mutual accountability, and serve as guiding lights for what we can become, even if we are not yet there. However, successful transformational change leaders never confuse aspiration with reality.

We may hope and plan to be better than we are today. And, we can put in place strategies and mechanisms to drive the changes we believe are essential to future success. But, our optimism about the future can never be allowed to cloud our judgment about today.

We are where we are. The situation is what it is. We must confront reality, and that process begins with understanding, acknowledging, and addressing what we are facing and what we need to do about it. Reality is the baseline for change. Aspiration is the roadmap to transformation. Reality *and* aspiration are joined at the hip.

Facts *and* Feelings

Most of us are predictable. We resist change unless it is absolutely necessary, and rely selectively on data and other evidence (or strong opinions) to sustain and protect the status quo. Often, we cite facts to sell the need for change as we see it, and refute or dismiss facts with which we disagree. The scientific term for this phenomenon is "human nature."

Then, wham. A new competitor, pandemic, or problem swoops in from what seems like another planet, disrupts our entire universe, and turns everything upside down. Was our data inaccurate? No, the facts are the facts. They may just be the wrong facts, focused on the wrong things, watched by the wrong people, addressed at the wrong time, and approached in the wrong way. Facts matter in leading transformational change.

But, what about feelings? Confidence or confusion. Engagement or entitlement. Humility or hubris. Pride or panic. Feelings are informed by facts, but they are formed by people. Facts provide the context for understanding the need to change, but feelings stimulate insights and action. The facts may tell us exactly what we need to do, but our feelings will dictate if and when we ever actually do it. The scale tells us we are overweight. Yet, do we feel compelled to transform ourselves through diet and exercise? Facts *and* feelings are the rocket fuel for leading transformational change.

Speed *and* Rhythm

How do we know whether we are driving transformational change too fast or too slowly? Can we answer this question based on how people feel about the change, whether they support or resist it, or if they understand it? Not exactly. Most victims of change think it is moving too fast, and most leaders of change believe it is moving too slowly. Both are probably right, based on their unique perspectives.

The speed of change can be directly correlated with the perceived need for it, clarity about it, level of resistance to it, availability of information and resources to address it, courage of those leading the effort to face it, engagement or disengagement of those being helped or victimized to participate in it, and many other factors. Speed of transformational change is not, in itself, a measure of success.

Speed must be accompanied by rhythm. As musicians might agree, playing a song faster, and getting to the end more quickly, does not by definition make the song better. The quality of the song is enhanced by rhythm – whether we pace the song as intended, play together in harmony, and keep everyone on the same sheet of music throughout the experience. Music is an apt metaphor for leading transformational change. It needs to happen at an appropriate speed, and with an agreed-upon and harmonious rhythm. Speed without rhythm is noise. Speed *and* rhythm in harmony make great music, and transformational change.

Flexibility *and* Focus

How crazy would it be if we tried to lead transformational change by being inflexible? Change, by definition, requires flexibility – at least enough to know what to change and when to change it. Successful transformational change also requires a willingness to experiment, test, adapt, adjust, reassess, practice, improve, solidify, and reinforce. By its nature, transformational change is about flexing to the need, at the right moment, and being agile enough to adjust course based on new information.

Yet, being flexible does not also mean being unclear or going with the flow. The worst change leaders I have been around try new stuff, see if it sticks, fail to learn from their mistakes, try something else, suddenly turn left without using their turn signal, drive around the block a few times, refuse to ask for directions or check the map, and end up right where they started – but, running late and highly frustrated. This is not flexibility, it is failure.

While being flexible is important to building agility and resilience, so too is focus. Do we understand the handful of most important things we are trying to achieve? Are we clear about what must be done first, second, and third? Can we resist the temptation to chase shiny objects, only do the fun and easy things, or bounce from new idea to new idea? Flexibility means we understand that there are multiple roads to drive to grandma's house, *and* focus is defined by showing up on time with the grandkids, despite holiday traffic.

Difference *and* Improvement

At the end of a long transformational change journey, what is our ultimate measure of success? Are we satisfied that things are different, or do we insist that our readiness, mindset, skillset, or performance have improved? Doing things differently is an important part of change. We let go of old and outdated practices and processes. We shift gears to new approaches, using new tools. We change something.

Changing things that do not matter may qualify as different. However, it is not better. Changing everything without knowing what made the real difference might feel like transformation. But, it is not improvement.

Yes, doing things differently qualifies as change. To meet the transformational change test, however, there must also be improvement. Knowing how to achieve difference *and* improvement is the name of the game. This insight leads us to our final paradox.

Change *and* Transformation

In Chapter 1, we identified four important questions that this book purports to answer, one of which is, "*Is it true that all transformation is change, but not all change is transformational?*" As we were beginning work on our book, this simple but powerful question was posed by my long-time business colleague and friend, Dr. John Boudreau, who is also a key contributor to the book (see John's essay, co-authored with Jonathan Donner, titled *Transformation Through Work Without Jobs*, in Chapter 5). As usual, John's insight and wisdom led us to the heart of the matter.

Some might argue that the concepts of change and transformation are redundant, essentially two ways of expressing the same thing. However, many contributors to this book, including me, argue there is an important difference between change and transformation. Change, while crucial, can be a minor tweak to something very specific. Transformation, on the other hand, implies and demands a much more comprehensive, systemic, sustainable, and likely disruptive set of alternatives and actions. And, in our way of thinking, it must lead to improvement.

This book acknowledges the value of tweaks *and* disruptions, as well as difference *and* improvement. As the book will make increasingly clear, leading transformational change must be about change *and* transformation!

Part II

Insights

Expert Perspectives (Essays) – Collective Wisdom

What do you get when more than two dozen experts contribute 25 essays on leading transformational change? A treasure trove of insights and collective wisdom, and a wide array of perspectives amid a sea of undeniably consistent advice. We have curated contributions from seven Chief HR Officers, one Chief Transformation Officer, and 20 expert consultants and academics – all with extensive experience and credentials in leading transformational change.

Every essay is unique. Areas of focus range from deeply personal challenges like confronting a life-threatening cancer diagnosis to reimagining the organizational and societal impact of a world of work without jobs (as we have traditionally defined them). You will learn about concepts and techniques such as engaging the mind, vulnerability moments, psychological safety, toxic positivity, adaptive leadership, intentionality, constructive disruption, influencers, experimentation, and a VUCA (Volatile, Uncertain, Complex, Ambiguous) world, among others.

Our contributing authors will tell you how to drive transformational change, one person at a time; go wider, farther, and deeper; engage in art-based dialogue and storytelling; define success, include everyone, and be transparent; build more resilient organizations; create change champions, positive energy, and usefulness; remaster the art of connection; foster more diverse and inclusive organizations; see around corners; capitalize on the employment lifecycle; develop a transformation playbook, and many more.

The angles on leading transformational change are diverse and rich, the lenses varied and vivid. But, despite the breadth of perspectives, every essay concludes with the same laser focus – **Three Things to Know or Do About Transformational Change**. Our formula is simple, "Think Big, Start Small, Move Fast," as described by Nicholas La Russo, MD, Barbara Spurrier, and Gianrico Farrugia, MD, in their book of the same name.[1]

Identify and explain a broad spectrum of ideas related to transformational change. Focus on a few highest-leverage priorities that will make the biggest difference to success. Lead transformational change with a sense of urgency,

DOI: 10.4324/9781003227137-6

and then act. Every essay, no matter what the topic, will help you figure out what to do about transformational change – proactively and pragmatically.

Taken holistically, the 25 essays in Chapters 3–5 of the book offer collective wisdom about leading transformational change. They are also organized according to three different perspectives:

1. Individuals (Chapter 3)
2. Teams (Chapter 4)
3. Organizations (Chapter 5)

While each essay addresses more than one of the above perspectives, all have a *primary* lens through which transformational change is examined. While no essay focuses primarily on a societal lens, it is worth emphasizing that *every* essay suggests implications for society at large – in addition to a more direct emphasis on individuals, teams, and/or organizations.

You may also note that the 25 essays are not evenly distributed among the Individual, Team, and Organizational perspectives. Contributing authors were asked to focus on the transformational change issues most important and interesting to them, thereby allowing us to understand their primary passions. The final score was eight essays about Individuals, four essays about Teams, and 13 essays about Organizations. Now, let us see how each expert plays the game of leading transformational change.

Note

1. Nicholas LaRusso, M.D., Barbara Spurrier, MHA, and Gianrico Farrugia, M.D., *Think Big, Start Small, Move Fast: A Blueprint for Transformation From the May Clinic Center for Innovation* (New York: McGraw Hill Education, 2015).

Chapter 3

Individuals

Engaging All Three Parts of the Mind to Achieve Transformational Change Buy-In (and Success)

By Dr. Beth Banks Cohn

When you introduce transformational change into an organization, each employee brings all three parts of their mind to it. That includes the Cognitive (knowledge, intelligence), Affective (emotions, motivation), and Conative (drive, instinctive action) parts of their mind. But, leaders often ignore this reality as they plan for change, missing out on opportunities to build success into their rollout plans. This essay builds on the research of Kathy Kolbe, the world's leading authority on human instincts.

Three Parts of the Mind and Change

Throughout history, philosophers and scholars believed that there were three parts of the mind: Cognitive, Affective, and Conative. As far back as Plato and Aristotle, there was recognition of these three ways we think, feel, and act. During the Age of Enlightenment, philosophers claimed that Reason was the sole basis for human action. This is systemically but unconsciously taught even today. Yet, engaging the three parts of the mind is essential for successful transformational change. Most people understand Cognitive and Affective, but Conative still remains outside the lexicon of most change initiatives. Let us look at how these three parts of the mind work during transformational change.

Cognitive

The Cognitive part of the mind is where our knowledge, IQ, skills, reason, experience, and education reside. This is the easiest part to measure. On the surface, it is easy to understand and easy to plan for.

DOI: 10.4324/9781003227137-7

Giving people knowledge and skills is part of almost every transformational change plan. On the surface that might seem like enough. "I explained the change. We trained them. So why aren't they adopting the new way of doing business?", a senior executive once asked me. WHY indeed.

Explaining the "what" at the organizational level is an important first step. However, employees also need to understand the WHY. Not only your WHY, but they also need to evaluate the facts for themselves. You hired smart people, but telling them to just accept what you are saying and get back to work (in the new way, of course) is not enough. You must engage the Cognitive part of the mind during change.

I once worked on the closing of a manufacturing plant that took three years to complete. Operations leadership had decided on this course of action over many months of deliberation and needed the plant employees to buy into it (even if they did not agree) in order to keep manufacturing quality products for the next three years. I encouraged the plant leaders to hold a series of sessions where they took the entire organization through a detailed explanation of how they came to their conclusion.

In preparation, I helped them create a change discussion guide that was filled with the business problem, the facts and stats that framed the decision, and the reasoning behind the decision. Every level had a chance to hear from Operations leadership, as well as from their own leadership in the plant. Senior and middle managers were engaged and prepared for all discussions. Everyone had a chance to participate. People were not happy with the decision, but understanding it at the Cognitive level was key to their acceptance.

Affective

The Affective part of the mind is where our emotions, motivation, attitudes, desires, preferences, and values reside. There are instruments that measure aspects of the Affective part of the mind such as DiSC, MBTI, and Strengths Finder, to name a few. These instruments help us understand ourselves better, but do not always help an organization plan for change.

Here is the key to helping employees manage through the emotions associated with the change: Employees must believe in an idea enough to sacrifice for it. This sacrifice might be time, energy, or even the job as they know it.

I once worked with an organization to merge two divisions together. All employees in positions of leadership, from supervisors through more senior leaders, had mixed feelings about this plan. Before creating a timeline for the merger, I had all leaders go through a series of conversations with their manager focusing on what they were losing, what they were gaining, what they were afraid of, and what it would take to get them on board with the change. These conversations were critical in gaining all the leadership support needed for the next step: having the same conversations with employees. The merger was successful in ways never anticipated, such as improved morale and higher levels of engagement. These results were associated with the part of the plan that focused on the Affective part of change.

Leaders must be willing to engage in conversations that help people get to the level of conviction needed to make the change an Affective success.

Conative

The Conative or the doing part of the mind is where drive, necessity, mental energy, innate force, talents, and instinct reside. The Conative part of the mind contains striving instincts that drive a person's natural way of taking action, making decisions, and creative problem-solving.

When a transformational change is announced, employees must be willing to devote their time and energy to participating in the process of change. This commitment will be lacking if employees are being asked to work against their grain, or against their instincts. Their mental energy will be depleted, and they will therefore have less to give. Productivity will drop.

I once worked with a company that so fundamentally changed certain jobs that the people in those jobs could not work. They were being asked to take action based on little facts, which went against the way they instinctively worked best. Work essentially came to a halt. Leadership created a new team with representatives from all levels to figure out what to do. Only when taking into consideration people's instinctive action was a solution and way forward found.

If you are in the middle of a change and cannot figure out why it is not moving faster or sticking the way you need it to, look to the Conative impact. You might find the answers you need to make adjustments and move forward.

Case Study: What the Three Parts of the Mind Look Like During Change

I worked with a sales force that was fundamentally changing the way they sold to their customers. Marketing leadership took a look at sales performance and decided that more consistent sales were needed across the board. They found a different sales methodology that guaranteed more consistent results and moved to implement it.

When I came on board, Sales and Marketing had announced the change and were planning on rolling it out immediately. Materials and formal training would come later, but in the beginning, the sales managers would be responsible for rolling it out to their teams. Materials were not ready yet, so sales reps would have to adopt their current sales materials for each customer.

I was brought onto the project because they expected a lot of resistance from their very mature and experienced sales force.

Cognitively, they were focused on skill-building within the new selling model but completely ignored the need to make sure people understood the why associated with the change so they would have a chance to evaluate and come to the same conclusion themselves.

Affectively, they did see resistance as a challenge but did not seem to understand why or how they might prevent it. They did not realize that their superstars would be "losing face" as their way of selling was discounted.

Conatively, they did not realize that they created a situation where sales reps' instincts and innate talents were being ignored. The amount of mental energy they would now need to do the same job was overwhelming.

The plan we ultimately created included all three parts of the mind. The pilot included experienced sales reps who used both their instincts and the new methodology to create success. Those sales reps used their new skills to teach and mentor others during the rollout.

The rollout did not start until the selling materials were ready to use. The plan included upskilling for sales managers, as well as the tools and skills they needed to mentor their teams using all three parts of the mind. During the pilot and regular rollout, there were also ample opportunities for individuals to participate in sessions where they could voice concerns and get answers to challenges they were facing.

The rollout of the new sales methodology was delayed by about four months to give the pilot time to conclude and to make tweaks to the methodology and sales aids. But the sales teams made up for that delay by meeting the year-end sales goal in the first six months, by using the new methodology.

Three Things to Know or Do About Transformational Change

1. Include the actions that take into account the Cognitive, Affective, and Conative parts of the mind.
2. If a change is not going well, use the three parts of the mind to diagnose what area to address.
3. Always include ways for 360° communication, and make changes accordingly based on what you learn.

The Role of the Learning Leader in Transforming Organizations

By Kelly Bean

Opportunities to execute transformational change in organizations have become more complex. As new jobs are created and the early career workforce ascends to leadership positions in organizations, a new challenge awaits. Will this workforce be ready to assume the leadership roles needed to navigate the transition of human/machine collaboration, algorithms, and other workplace challenges? How will the organizational culture transform to support the acquisition, development, and retention of talent? Will organizations provide lifelong learning opportunities to continue upskilling the workforce as technology advances? What roles do leaders across the organization need to assume?

This essay will examine how focusing on individual leader development accelerates team and, thus, organizational impact. We will look at the development of individuals, the roles leaders must play, and the achievable outcomes that await learning leaders to be the levers of transformation.

What Is a Learning Leader?

Learning. Leadership. Transformation. These words, and so many others, have become part of the daily vocabulary in organizations. Yet, having spent the last two decades engaging with thousands of executives and senior leaders from hundreds of organizations around the globe, I have found a few common threads as they pertain to individual growth:

- *Learning is a journey*
- *It takes time to shift a mindset*
- *Practice through intentional reflection and challenge leads to results*

Leaders need to be learners, and learners are leaders. Therefore, the goal of creating a future talent pipeline that is ready to take on the challenges of complexity is to create a learning leader.

The learning leader demonstrates their capabilities by performing through three integrated lenses:

1. **Strategy and Data**
2. **Organizational and Individual Leadership**
3. **Global Trends and Social Awareness**

Learning leader effectiveness sits at the intersection of these three capability lenses. Individual performance is enabled through leaders. Here are seven critical roles learning leaders play:

1. Innovator
2. Value Creator
3. Growth Catalyst
4. Translator
5. Change Activist
6. Communicator
7. Agile Problem Solver

Divided into these three groups, each role subset has its own responsibilities (see Figure 3.1):

*   **Innovators and Value Creators**
*   **Growth Catalysts and Translators**
*   **Change Activists, Communicators, and Agile Problem Solvers**

Often these roles are played simultaneously, or a few of them at one time. If you do not play a role for a while, it is like a muscle in atrophy. For example, you may be a strong communicator, but when those strengths are challenged with new perspectives, the muscle needs to be redeveloped or maybe even reshaped.

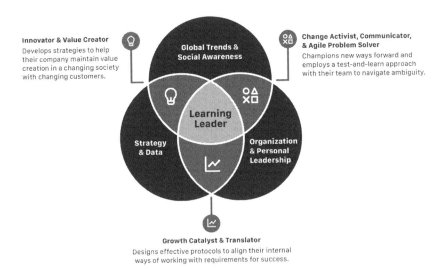

Figure 3.1 Learning Leader Venn diagram (Bean, 2019).

Learning is a continuous and lifelong journey. Learning and development opportunities, formal and informal, provide the intentional and safe space for reflection and challenge. As we develop learning leaders to perform in their roles and expand their capabilities, we see the growth of the individual and the teams they lead.

Learning and Development Designed to Support Transformational Change

As a learning leader, there is no shortage of learning and development partners to choose from as you embark on developing the talent in your organization. And, most likely, you need a little bit from each of your leaders to create an integrated learning experience for all. For example, early in my career leading university-based executive education, I had an experience at UCLA with my children that changed how I thought about learning and development.

Both of my young sons were diagnosed with developmental delays and had the excellent opportunity to participate in a program at UCLA targeted at two- to seven-year-olds. My kids were two and three at the time and received speech, sensory integration, physical therapy, behavioral therapy, etc. As a parent team, my husband and I managed each of those providers individually. We did our best to explain to each service partner what was happening in the support silos. But, something was missing, and the kids were not growing, despite the expert guidance.

Something changed when we arrived at UCLA and had these new support partners working together collectively every day. Our children responded in ways we never thought possible. A pathway for performance and potential emerged. New skills were learned, and a developmental mindset was created. Their training was integrated, intentional, and reflective, and the performance and growth came at the intersections of the providers' support. All hands meetings took place multiple times during the week. The care team, with laser focus, made decisions on intentional experiences that each would reinforce through their expertise. The skill-building was delivered through the lens of their expertise, but the intervention was collaborative. No one person could provide the growth runway, and it was not a speech issue or an occupational therapy issue; it was a let us develop the "whole" child challenge.

This approach struck me to my core as a learning professional and has stayed with me to this day. We miss the opportunity for growth when we only develop skills, and we miss the chance to magnify performance when we only focus on growth. Since this experience, I have put integration and development, and the intersections of capabilities, at the forefront of developing others to lead individual and organizational change. Here are a few points to keep in mind as you are designing learning and development experiences to support transformational change:

- *Balance the polarity of action and reflection*
- *Meet the learner where they are, not where you are*
- *Create challenging experiences in a safe place*
- *Remember that context is the key*
- *Simplify the complexity*

How Intentional Leader Development Drives Individual and Organizational Transformation

The Cohort Approach: A large home improvement retailer customized a high-potential leadership program for their director-level store and support center managers. As part of the four-month learning journey, participants engaged in executive coaching, assessment, simulations, action learning, and classroom sessions. The cohort built a strong bond, and with a shared language, cascaded their learning to others in the organization at the store level. A focus of the program was on developing others to have an operational excellence mindset. The CEO commented on the program's success when he witnessed store employees using the program's language during his store visits. As a result, the company embraced operational excellence, and growth accelerated. Participants in that program continued to receive C-Suite promotions with the firm, and many are now leading other organizations in the C-Suite after a long tenure. The company also prides itself on many store-level associates being promoted to management and leadership positions.

An Intact Executive Leadership Team: Five intact community health center leadership team members participated in a 12-month learning journey that focused on building a strategic and business mindset and becoming a high-performing team. During the 12 months, participants worked together on an action learning project that dealt with branding their centers in the community, building strategic plans, and enhancing their team's communication and leadership skills. The results positioned the 12 participating center teams to be value-based healthcare delivery pillars in their communities. The centers, now a decade past the implementation of the Affordable Care Act, have proven to be steadfast as both employers and providers of choice in the communities they serve. Common language and a patient, intentional focus on leading the business, self, and others solidified these crucial providers of the social determinants of health.

A High-Potential Team Leader Accelerates to the C-Suite: An individual leader participated in three rounds of executive coaching over six years while being promoted and given developmental assignments at various organizations. The focus of development was on leading others and leading peers. The high-potential-turned CEO has led the turnaround of three $1 billion plus organizations. This leader always delivered results, no matter what, yet the execution path was brutal for those on the team. Focusing on vertical development, including reflection, coaching, feedback, and mentoring, accelerated this leader to new levels. Recently, this leader spoke to a new client about how team, communication, and purpose are the most important skills you can have as a CEO leading transformation. When asked what the turning point was in his development, the answer was listening to others and being willing to be vulnerable.

Leaders lead. They set the tone for leader development, and for transformational change.

Three Things to Know or Do About Transformational Change

1. *Practice, practice, practice.*
2. *Be patient.*
3. *Celebrate the challenges that you outgrow.*

Leading Transformational Change During Vulnerability Moments: An Opportunity to Shine

By Rebecca Feder

A willingness to change often starts with establishing trust and engagement well before the shift is needed. During times of uncertainty, people feel vulnerable, which can provide leaders with an opportunity to shine.

Most people's first reaction to transformational change is that it is hard. Even when people believe in the value of the proposed change, they often worry about the impact on themselves and others, or they struggle to find the time and mind space to process what they need to do differently. This disruption creates an opportunity for leaders who, through natural tendencies or learned behavior, run toward the change versus away. They lean in and see the future state as exciting or the process as an opportunity to learn something new. These leaders become role models, showing a different mindset and inviting others to follow by showing the change is possible.

When an employee needs help at work, for whatever reason, and a manager or other colleagues show up in a meaningful way, the person is more likely to be engaged once things settle down for them. However, too often, either the employee does not feel comfortable showing that they are struggling, or they are not given the help they need. Either scenario can lead to an undesirable outcome. We call these pivotal times "vulnerability moments." Think about times when you have been vulnerable and how it felt when people did or did not help you.

Historically, vulnerability moments have often been individual: a stretch role, balancing raising kids with careers, caring for elders, dealing with acts of social injustice, managing a health crisis, getting divorced, etc. There have also been times when people in the United States have felt a collective sense of vulnerability as well: Kennedy's assassination, the Challenger explosion, 9/11, or local communities working their way through a natural disaster, mass shooting, or other tragic events.

During the 2020–2021 pandemic, people were dealing with the health implications of COVID-19, difficult conversations about the impacts of social distancing at senior centers and schools, job loss and remote work, and other stressors such as social injustice, the declining environment, and polarized politics. Even the good moments like having a baby or buying a house may have felt difficult when experiencing them without loved ones around to celebrate. The stressors lasted for a somewhat prolonged period of time and most people felt a real sense of unease, loss, or isolation at some point.

These vulnerability moments gave leaders a chance to connect with people on a more personal level and work together to find meaningful solutions. Let us look at an example:

> Shoban and his wife work full-time and have four young kids and a grandfather living with them. Their childcare options dissolved due to COVID-19. The mom is part of a union that was called back to work so Shoban needed to figure out how to work from home while caring for the kids and elder.
>
> His manager was able to arrange work for him that could mostly be done in the evenings or weekends, although there were also some core-hour commitments that Shoban was able to work around. There was flexibility on both sides and open, honest conversation. Yet, even with these accommodations, it was hard for Shoban to perform at full capacity during this period.
>
> Shoban's manager saw his employee's request for help as an opportunity to engage, not as a burden. Simply shifting the schedule would have been enough. However, the style with which Shoban's manager responded let him know that his contributions are valued, his personal life is important, and the organization is investing in him for the long term.
>
> Shoban and his manager trust each other and are able to have authentic, transparent discussions at a different level than before the pandemic. Shoban reports feeling loyal, confident he can manage through chaos and ambiguity, and more ready to lead change knowing his manager will have his back.

What can you do, big or small, to build trust ahead of time to help people prepare for transformational change?

Trusted leaders who were able to manage their teams through change during the pandemic stood out by delivering results when the companies most needed them. An organization's change initiatives can be led by leaders at all levels. Let us take a look at the roles of peer team members, managers, and senior leaders.

Peer team members are often an overlooked yet very important group when it comes to engagement and building the foundation for change.

Strong peer team members:

- Lead by example to show commitment, not just compliance. They do their part for the organization and customers even when it is not easy
- Help create the environment where they want to work versus waiting for someone else to initiate
- Are honest when they need support which allows others to ask for help more easily in return when they need it, and they proactively ask about the needs of others
- Collaborate with and proactively learn from colleagues

- Focus on team success which includes challenging, encouraging, and advocating for colleagues so they perform better

Due to their relationships with employees and decision-making authority, managers play a critical role in organizations – arguably the most important role during times of uncertainty.

Strong managers:

- Select and develop team members with the will and skill to create a positive team experience. Bringing the right people onto the team is critical, as is providing honest feedback about their performance and interactions with others
- Stay connected to individual team members in meaningful ways to create an environment where people have a sense of belonging. And, they understand their team members' personal and professional goals in order to best support them
- Are people leaders who represent the needs of employees to senior leaders
- Ensure commitments are met through the strong performance of the team

Strong senior leaders:

- Create a vision people believe in and instill a culture of inclusion
- Select and develop people leaders with the will and skill to effectively engage their team members
- Encourage policies and practices across the organization that enable engagement and transformational change

When people are vulnerable and get the support they need from peers, managers, and senior leaders, there is a stronger emotional commitment. My crowdsourcing efforts have revealed this commitment occurs when a person feels a sense of purpose and belonging so they can bring their whole self to work. In turn, this energy enables the discretionary effort needed to lean into the transformational change that drives excellent business results.

As Mahatma Gandhi said, "Be the change you want to see in the world."

Three Things to Know or Do About Transformational Change

1. Notice "vulnerability moments" in others because they provide an opportunity for a leader to show up in a meaningful way. Invite colleagues to be more engaged, once things settle down for them. This can be the first step in establishing trust and comfort for future change management.

2. In 2020–2021, COVID-19 created a somewhat unusual collective sense of vulnerability and allowed companies an opportunity to accelerate their support for employees and transformational change abilities. Those lessons are still valuable reminders even after companies have settled into a new normal.

3. Trusted leaders at all levels who were able to manage their teams through change during the pandemic stood out by delivering results when companies and employees most needed them.

What Does a Life-Threatening Cancer Have to Do With Transformational Change?

By Marisa Harris

You may be asking yourself: "What does a life-threatening cancer have to do with me?" What if I said there are universal principles of success that can transform *any* challenge regardless of its kind? What if I said that at some point everyone will experience a moment in life that seems to change everything they counted on?

I went on this journey in 1998 before I knew anyone who understood that a health challenge could be strategically transformative. My experience taught me that we have an essential choice when challenging events happen. We can choose to resist them and back away. Or we can be an active agent and use these events to grow. I chose the latter, which was chronicled in the book, *FULFILLED! Critical Choices: Work, Home, Life,* by William A. Schiemann.[1]

I had been part of an executive team that just transformed a mediocre company into number one in its industry by using a new business success model, the Balanced Scorecard. Then shockingly, I was diagnosed with stage four pancreatic cancer and was told nothing could be done; I had at best nine months to live! I expected that if I found the best physicians and followed their instructions, I would get well. Initially, I accepted their verdict. Then, I heard this voice, "Marisa, you can give up and die or get creative."

I decided to apply this same business success process to my greatest desire – to get well again. I had a vision: *I'm going to see my three daughters get married.* Instantly, I moved from hopelessness to enormous optimism. I had a plan. I started sharing my positivity and my plan with others at work. Many were skeptical about my beating pancreatic cancer. Others lined up with my strategy, offering useful resources and valuable introductions.

Not only did I get well, but a new career as a cancer coach blossomed out of what looked like the worst possible situation. The first step in transforming my results was unlearning some things which had worked for me in the past concerning health challenges: to solely rely on doctors and medicine. I decided to learn and incorporate some new ways of thinking and acting from others who had achieved extraordinary results against all odds.

You may say that I was one of the lucky ones that beat the statistics. As I worked with other leaders, however, I found that the lessons I learned are valuable and worth passing on. Here is the story of one leader with great business attributes who also did not realize that these lessons could be applied to a personal health situation. Nor did he imagine that his health challenge would be transformational for him and his organization.

Scott Moore is the CEO of Kidango, the largest provider of pre-school education to children who need it most in the Bay Area. In 2018, Kidango was engaged in a major strategic change that would shift their measurement of success from growing revenue to focusing on the impact that they were having on children's readiness for kindergarten.

In the midst of this strategic change, Scott was diagnosed with pancreatic cancer. He had tremendous fear around dying, about not being able to be a dad to his 14-year-old son, and about not being able to lead Kidango. How was he going to go through harsh treatment and fulfill his duties?

Scott made the decision to focus his attention on getting well. He clearly knew that he needed help, and inspired by my story and approach, he reached out to me for coaching.

There were many choices that Scott made. The most important one was to recognize the seriousness of this diagnosis, while also needing to build his confidence in his ability to get well. Given that he would be getting very strong chemotherapy followed by surgery and more chemotherapy, he realized that he would not be able to fulfill all his duties as CEO. He decided not to keep his condition a secret.

He informed his board, leadership team, and employees. In celebration of New Year's Eve, December 31, 2018, Scott wrote an email to all employees, thanking them for all the cards, gifts, and words of encouragement. He told them that he had started chemotherapy and was responding well. The effect of his communication was to engage the hearts and minds of the people who worked for Kidango, and even the children and families. They felt trusted and inspired by his sharing and were willing to let go of old roles and step into new ones that would drive the new strategic plan.

While Scott and I worked on creating his vision of getting well again, and on aligning his thoughts and actions with his vision, he was also growing his confidence in the capabilities of his leadership team and staff. His expectation was that Kidango would continue to serve the children and make progress on the new goals. He was surprised and delighted that every one of the strategic goals was met and even surpassed.

Upon reflection, Scott realized that he had transformed his vision about what it would take to be a leader who created and drove strategic change in Kidango. Because of his decision to make getting well his number one priority, his executive team now fulfilled his strategic leadership role. They not only drove the work but developed the strategic goals. Scott was still engaged, but his role as a leader became more advisory. Interestingly, he felt more deeply connected to his team, the employees, and even the children.

What were the benefits of the cancer diagnosis for the organization? It opened the doorway for people to connect with Kidango in a more caring way. They had called themselves a family prior to the diagnosis. Now they were acting as one. Scott put it this way, "Even the CEO needs help! It showed that we are all in this together and that we all care about each other."

Everyone rose to the occasion because of "trust." People trusted that if they got sick or a loved one did, they would get paid during time off. The trust that they would be supported led to extraordinary outcomes for the children and families Kidango served, and also for all employees.

Business performance metrics reflected the benefits of Scott's actions. Turnover was down. The learning gains were so impressive that the *New York Times* wrote an article attesting to the impressive learning gains of Kidango's children. As the COVID-19 pandemic emerged, an additional benefit surfaced. The employees' response to the pandemic was built on their experience of supporting the CEO. Kidango did not close down. They were determined to stay open. In contrast to the majority of young children in the United States, Kidango's students experienced minimal learning loss.

Scott's decision to disclose that he had cancer differs from that of many executives, who either keep it a secret or communicate in a way that is vague and even misleading. Often this choice comes from a perception that disclosure will lead to being pushed aside. In my experience, however, it is almost always the case that people will rally to your side. Most often, you can continue to play a vital role, especially in providing new growth opportunities.

The heart of this story is not about Scott's cancer, but about what it led to and how it changed the organization. Scott learned that the most important step a leader can take to ensure successful and lasting transformational change is to let go and trust your people. Allow them to rise to the occasion and allow them to care about you.

Three Things to Know or Do About Transformational Change

1. Start with an assessment of where you are now. This includes an examination of external challenging events and the impact they have on you, your family, and your organization. External savvy also requires an awareness of your internal world. This awareness of your perceptions, beliefs, and biases is what allows you to access other viewpoints and enables you to judge situations clearly and effectively.
2. People who overcome the most unfortunate circumstances elect to go through this journey from a place of choice and self-determination. They decide that since this difficult challenge has happened, life has selected them to go through it for their own growth as well as for the growth of others, and they take it on as a personal challenge.
3. Trust is essential for getting people aligned and engaged with change initiatives. Modeling and inspiring trust is the first step to building a community that comes together and stays together regardless of the challenges.

Seven Ways to Cultivate Intentional Leadership

By Dr. Orly Maravankin

In my executive coaching practice, leaders often share that they feel over-whelmed in the face of constant demands and complex challenges. It is easy to see why they feel that way. Without the space to pause and reflect, without the skills to navigate in an unpredictable world, many feel anxious and stuck.

Today's world is characterized by Volatility, Uncertainty, Complexity, and Ambiguity (VUCA). In a VUCA world, leaders cannot control the pace of transformational change, predict what will happen, or avoid distractions. To operate well in that space, leaders need to cultivate a different mindset and adopt new practices. That, in turn, requires being deliberate about how they think and what they do. This essay will explore four keys to intentional leader-ship, why it is critical in today's environment, and specific ways to cultivate these capabilities.

Four Keys to Intentional Leadership

- *Aligning your behavior with your values and purpose:* Alignment is the congruence between who you are, what you want, and how you act. To understand how aligned you are, begin by exploring the following ques-tions. Do you have a clear and compelling vision for your team or organi-zation? Do you act in a way that is aligned with your values and supports your vision? In my coaching practice, I meet many leaders who are not aligned. Alignment helps bring clarity and focus, expanding the limits that were holding you back.

- *Managing your emotional triggers*: Triggering situations often threaten our basic psychological needs for safety, status, autonomy, and connec-tion. When that happens, negative emotions arise making it hard for us to think clearly. Not managed, negative emotions cause us to be reactive and impulsive, and to ruminate by mentally rehearsing what is wrong. Self-management skills are critical because in order to effectively lead others, leaders first need to lead themselves. When you regulate your triggers, it opens the space for you to act based on choice. You role-model the behav-iors you want to see in others by showing up the way you want to more consistently.

- *Managing your focus and energy:* A key challenge many leaders complain about is lack of quality time to think. Focused attention and energy man-agement are critical leadership skills, especially in a VUCA world. When leaders' attention wanders and when their energy is drained, they are not at their peak performance. As a leader, becoming aware of what you pay attention to and understanding your energy drainers is a prerequisite to your ability to effectively manage your time, and to recharge.

- *Taking responsibility for your own growth:* Constant change requires continuous learning. Being deliberate about your growth involves shifting your mindset from "knowing" to "learning." It means, for example, reflecting on everyday occurrences as learning opportunities with a *growth mindset* to further develop yourself. It also means seeking diverse perspectives and being open-minded to consider contrarian points of view to expand your horizons. And, it involves cultivating a *beginner's mindset*, pursuing new experiences to foster your growth and creativity.

How Can You Become an Intentional Leader?

Zoom Out to See the "Big Picture"

Asking yourself questions such as "what am I focusing on?" "what really matters in light of our values?" and "what's the mission of the organization?" will help you avoid being distracted by unimportant elements. It also allows you to review unchallenged assumptions and see hidden patterns. While both zooming in and zooming out are important for a full picture, a close-up view can sometimes get people stuck in the details. Bringing intentionality to the lenses you use serves as a reminder that you lead in service of a purpose larger than yourself.

My client Marla, a Regulatory Affairs executive at a pharmaceutical company, purposely adopted patient lenses whenever she had to make tough budget decisions. That perspective also enabled her to weather the storms she continuously faced by focusing on her higher purpose.

Build Your Self-Awareness and Self-Management Muscle

When you know yourself and your "why" for being, it becomes easier to lead while remaining true to your core values. Spending time in reflection and seeking input from others are great tools to build your self-awareness. Self-awareness is also necessary for your ability to self-manage. Remaining calm under pressure allows you to think clearly and make good decisions, and it has a ripple effect on others. To self-manage, start by observing yourselves in real time, noticing what is happening, and labeling your emotions. Labeling is a basic mindfulness tool that has a powerful effect on quieting the mental chatter and creating clarity.

For example, take Jack, a brilliant marketer who was referred to me for coaching because he was considered impossible to work with. For him, building skills to regulate his emotional outbursts literally saved his job. It also shifted his CEO's perceptions of what is in store for Jack, who went from almost being fired to getting promoted to the C-level.

Take Pauses

One of the most powerful techniques to cultivate intentionality is simply to pause and reflect, creating the space to think and make intentional choices. It provides a mental and emotional reset. There are *in-the-moment* pauses you can take when you are triggered. Pausing intentionally to observe yourself in real time and notice your thoughts, feelings, and narratives helps to calm down stress levels. It also creates room for you to evaluate whether our judgments and conclusions are a product of proven or unverified assumptions and distorted interpretations.

There are also *purposeful pauses* you can build into your daily calendar to re-evaluate your priorities and help you focus on the best thing to do. It is a muscle you can build to consciously manage what you pay attention to, and over time, it will enable you to replace habits that derail you with more effective ones. The more ritualized the process is, the higher the likelihood of success.

Practice Retrospective Reflections

Retrospective reflections help leaders to build processes to refine, improve, and discover new solutions. They create the space to step back and examine the big picture. Furthermore, when you routinely engage in after-action reflections, you build the muscle to also notice what is happening when you are in the middle of action.

Commit to New Learning

In a complex world, it is difficult to have foresight. That is tough on our brains, which are hard-wired to seek certainty, rush to solutions in an attempt to achieve that certainty, and create mental shortcuts to process new information. Today's scope of demands and the pace of change further accelerate the brain's tendency to hasten and fix things.

Being intentional about new learning involves overcoming your "inner voices of resistance" and suspending judgment. It requires openness and willingness not to be in control, not be right, and not judge. In other words, it requires a shift in attitude from avoiding discomfort to making friends with it. Adopting a process that deliberately engages diverse perspectives helps mitigate the risk of over-simplification, and it sparks new ideas.

Commit to Experimentation

In a VUCA world, our past experience has a limited value in projecting the future. So when a problem requires multiple lenses and no clear solutions, experimentation allows you to step into unknown situations and keep your wits. Through experimentation, you can explore emerging possibilities, move fast, and course correct.

Seek Input and Feedforward Suggestions From Stakeholders

When you commit to an iterative process of self-development through seeking feedforward suggestions on how to improve, you become a better leader. You can start simply by identifying one or two focus areas you want to develop, and then solicit input from others.

Three Things to Know or Do About Transformational Change

1. Transformational leaders are particularly needed in a VUCA world. They provide a compelling purpose and vision to move forward in a complex, chaotic environment. They help others transcend beyond their own self-interests for the benefit of the group.
2. Intentionality is at the core of being a transformational leader, helping you become the best version of yourself leading others. Leaders can cultivate intentionality by zooming out to consider the big picture, building self-awareness, taking pauses, practicing retrospective reflections, committing to learning and experimentation, and seeking input.
3. Intentional leaders are aligned with their purpose, focused on the big picture, and deliberate in their choices. Leading themselves, they are focused on what matters most and as a result, they navigate more effectively through difficult situations. Leading others, they empower, inspire, and create resonant cultures where people can thrive.

Driving Transformational Change, One Person at a Time

By Alan May

With the proliferation of communications portals, the ubiquity of social media, and the explosion of data, it is increasingly difficult to break through the clutter and grab people's attention. Even harder is influencing individual change, which is the root of transformation.

Companies that approach change through the lens of those affected are the most successful in breaking through. This essay highlights best practices in driving transformational change, one person at a time.

Meet Maria

Maria awakens from deep sleep to her alarm at 6:00 AM and rolls over to look at her phone. She scans the texts received from her sister overnight regarding a health matter with their father and snaps off a response. Maria then picks up her "biz cell" and quickly skims a list of work emails she received while sleeping. Toggling between her two phones, she sees alerts from Twitter, Instagram, and Facebook along with top headlines from her preferred news sources. A headline about a social justice matter of deep concern to her prompts a quick review of two news articles and a video report. Having absorbed the headlines, Maria deletes a slew of "junk" emails in her personal inbox.

The daily communication overload has begun, and it is only 6:04 AM.

As part of her normal routine to reduce stress, Maria heads to the gym and sees a flyer on each locker about a policy change regarding the availability and price of Pilates classes. She ignores the notice because she does not have the time to assess the information and make a decision. After 30 minutes of intense cardio, she gets ready for work and stops by her local coffee shop. Her typical barista is not there. Where is Sam who knows her order by heart? On the way to the office, she realizes construction has finally started on the highway, after months of delays, detours, and false starts. It feels like everything is changing. . .

At work, Maria opens her laptop. The company intranet hails the implementation of the new vendor management system. One of her 64 unread emails is a missive from her boss reporting costs are headed in the wrong direction. Message: it is imperative they change things up, now!

Maria's first meeting is a company-wide all hands, regarding the massive operational model transformation that will change how they go to market and reposition their services to customers. The CEO barks out that all employees must change to accelerate the new operational model or the firm will fall behind its competitors. Sigh, another "existential threat," another company transformation, and another call for "change" with little context for what this means for Maria.

Why the Individual View Is Foundational to Drive Organizational Change

Given this cacophony, how can we expect Maria to even pay attention to "organizational change"? When everything seems to be changing, how can Maria keep up? How can she know what matters to her? Even more challenging is influencing individual change, which is the often-overlooked crux of a successful transformation.

Meaningful and sustainable organizational change is ultimately rooted in individual change – engagement, absorption, reflection, and action. As Maria experienced in just the first two hours of her day, change, information, and data are everywhere. She has no choice but to filter all the inputs, and ultimately decide where to place her attention and energy.

Inevitably, personal concerns will rise to the top – messages from family and friends, news and social posts on topics of personal interest, and issues of immediate concern. Only then will corporate priorities potentially gain some "share of mind."

Companies that approach change through the lens of those affected are the most successful in breaking through, inspiring individuals, and thus driving transformational change. I have seen countless leaders underestimate the personal side of change. People are dynamic, complex, and appropriately self-centered. Corporate change agendas are often abstract, non-linear, and frankly, boring. Achieving transformational success is dependent on leading and communicating in a way that acknowledges personal perspectives and emotions.

While there are many methods to engage both "hearts and heads," here are a few fundamentals that are particularly impactful in driving change.

Set a High Bar on Scope and Importance

Companies often announce transformation with blinders on, with multiple change initiatives competing as *the* most important. As a result of silos, change initiatives are designed with the view that each initiative bears equal weight. When change is approached in this manner, employees become numb, ignore conventional "management of change" techniques, and overlook what matters.

Organizations that prioritize their communication and change management efforts are the most successful in driving transformations – when it really matters.

Get Buy-In Through Humility

Some organizations wait too long to introduce transformations because they want to have all answers and plans "buttoned-up." Taking this approach poses a significant disadvantage by missing the most critical step in driving individual change: **gaining buy-in.** True buy-in is achieved when you bring employees on the journey with the humility that nobody has all the answers. Here is how you start:

1. *Share the reason behind the need to change first.* Employees want to know the "why" first. Starting with the "how" leaves employees feeling like the change is happening *to* them versus *with* them.
2. *Share the end state of where the transformation needs to take you,* with a compelling reason of why change needs to happen. We know we need to change because of X and we need to get to Y, together.
3. *Then, elicit help and ideas* by creating mechanisms for idea sharing across all levels of the organization. Consider internal social platforms, listening sessions, and voluntary "action teams" that can formulate ideas and provide input. Not everyone will participate, but employees will know they had the opportunity to offer their voice.

Communicate Frequently and Authentically

This may seem basic, but many organizations get it wrong. Once you have completed the foundational steps above, communication is king. Wash, rinse, repeat when it comes to communicating change. Research shows that you must communicate something on average seven times before action is taken. In my experience, that is an underestimation, and the key is using a multi-channel approach. Leverage emails, videos, meetings, and blogs, and try using non-traditional channels and methods like social media, chat groups, and "open mike" sessions.

Change is personal, so communication on achieving milestones, and setbacks (yes, that is critical, too), **should feel personal.** Organizations and leaders can do this by sharing updates and requests through channels like video and meetings where employees can see leaders, and by using an authentic, human tone, rather than corporate speak. Acknowledge that change is challenging but inspire employees along the way by reminding them about what is at stake, and what can be achieved. Use plain language. Tell stories. Celebrate the behaviors that drive outcomes.

Making change personal also means **making change social.** The more you get employees talking about change, the more they begin to understand it and act on it. Not just individually with supervisors, but in lateral groups.

At HPE, we encourage discussions around our change efforts by providing discussion guides and meeting outlines to help leaders start a dialogue with their teams, without pages of FAQs where we pretend to have all the answers. We host "kick the tires" sessions where we invite our top leaders to share ideas and concerns related to our transformation efforts. Starting at the top helps leaders build the muscle of encouraging "social" conversations where employees can grapple with what change means to them, and how they can contribute.

Celebrate and Recognize Individual Success

When sharing progress on milestones, start with personal recognition and celebrate individual and team behavior. Too often, leaders talk about achievements without putting a face to who made them happen. Make change personal by recognizing who drove the change, what challenges they overcame, and what behaviors they exhibited. Driving a personal view on change helps others relate to it and aspire to contribute in the same way.

In our current business reality, there is no end state with change. Great, you achieved your latest transformation, but there is likely another big change around the corner. To battle change fatigue, pause and celebrate once your transformation is achieved. Go big and be vivid. Employees will remember it the next time you ask them to get on board with a transformation.

Neuroscience tells us that change is processed through the same part of the brain as pain. Driving organizational change is not brain surgery, but it does require leaders to think through the eyes of individuals, like Maria. Taking a personal approach to implementing change is the key to transformational success.

Three Things to Know or Do About Transformational Change

1. Companies that approach change through the lens of those affected are most successful in breaking through.
2. Transformations should be designed through the lens of individuals and start by emphasizing scope and gaining buy-in.
3. Authentic, multi-channel communications are key to keeping employees engaged and ready to contribute to change.

Leading Change With Constructive Disruption

By Eva Sage-Gavin

On the eve of the new decade, we had high hopes for the "roaring 20's." Instead, we are living through a perfect storm of transformational change: COVID-19 has upended the way we live, how we work, and the way we view the future. Faced with unprecedented upheaval, companies are beginning to question past beliefs about their goals, strategies, and culture. As leaders and as humans, it is critical that we face these challenges with eyes wide open.

It is time to engage in constructive disruption.

What Is Constructive Disruption?

Disruptors, in the sense of startups and bold entrepreneurs, have long been hailed as integral to innovation. As agents of change, they shake things up, create what is new or bold, and move organizations forward in a dynamic way.

The pandemic shifted our focus in unexpected ways. We needed to find ways to deal not only with major business and technology challenges, but also with very human challenges, including mental health, work–life balance, and more. It makes the time ripe not just for disruption, but for "constructive disruption:" a process of change that raises up everyone involved. It is about reimagining how things can work better in the future, instead of relying on historic data or "the way it has always been done."

My first experience of "constructive disruption" was in middle school, when I was told woodshop and metalwork classes were "not for girls." But I watched the way my single mom had learned to do home repairs and saw how those life skills were invaluable. So I pressed . . . until they let me in. I got an A and took notice that the door swung open for others who wanted to take non-traditional classes. This experience represents the heart of constructive disruption.

Find out what you are missing, see a future need no one else is acknowledging, diverge from the predictable course to meet it, and in the process, help others benefit. For leaders guiding teams through the transformational change of the post-pandemic era, it is a roadmap to making the most of these extraordinary times.

To embrace constructive disruption, leaders must use technology, human ingenuity, and strong values to pursue the changes they want to see in their business and in the world. Here is how to do that.

Learn From the Future

Hindsight is 20/20, but true vision means looking forward and anticipating what comes next. Many say that the best way to predict the future is to create it yourself, and for constructive disruptors seeking transformational change, the time is now. That means leaders need to become futurists of sorts, adapting to changes before they happen to meet needs that are not yet known.

The best way to do this? Look to the data.

Predictive analytics can tell you more about the future of your company and industry than any crystal ball. We have more consumer data and better AI than ever before; in it, we find the opportunities for breakthroughs. When sales data changes, what are the implications not just for this quarter, but for a decade down the road? What can Census data tell us about customers years before they are ready for our products? Using current trends and strategic thinking enables us to know where we should pivot now to be best positioned in the future.

The challenge is to glean personal, human insights from an unprecedented flood of data and AI. We are in the midst of a massive workforce shakeup, with millions of workers leaving their jobs. The pandemic forced many to ask themselves, *Am I doing what I love? Am I living the way I want? Am I caring for my family and myself the way I should?* For nearly half of the workforce, the stunning answer was: No. And that is a transformational crisis of epic magnitude. Businesses that leverage data and insights on worker behavior and attitudes, and adapt to meet their needs, are the ones best positioned to engage the best of the labor pool, and in the process, create a better and more satisfying work environment for their employees.

See the Unseen Potential

For me, it always comes back to talent and people. Leaders who grow employee skills and in turn their business take a human-centered approach. They reimagine how work can be performed and reassess the changing skills needed to compete. For example, even as companies in 2021 reported difficulties in hiring for open positions, research suggests that the United States had 27 million "hidden workers," many of whom have the talent and potential to fill those roles but have been screened out via automated recruiting processes and other hurdles.

Harvard Business School Professor Joseph Fuller's Hidden Worker project[2] hinges on the idea that accessing untapped pools of valuable talent requires businesses to rethink their hiring strategies, replacing the search for the "perfect candidate" in favor of a targeted, skills and experience-based approach. Likewise, the Aspen Institute's Upskill America initiative[3] has worked for a decade to foster business–educational partnerships that connect capable talent to skill-building programs. These programs embody constructive disruption: Instead of abandoning those who do not fit a traditional mold, they create new paths to success and foster a culture that allows us to see the whole human, not just keywords on a resume. Individuals and businesses become more resilient as a result.

Embrace the Wisdom of the Group

Predictive insights can guide change, they just do not always come from where you would expect. In my time as a retail senior executive, we found the best sources of innovative ideas for kids' clothing were not always experienced designers, but the moms we brought in to test the apparel, who had a working insight of what was too scratchy, too difficult to snap, too flimsy. The best information on sales trends and localized price adjustments for a beverage corporation came from the truck drivers and bottlers, who could see the ground-level view of what consumers wanted and how they behaved.

In his book, *Superminds: The Surprising Power of People and Computers Thinking Together*, MIT professor Thomas Malone says it is not the individual who drives success, but rather groups of people coming together with a diversity of backgrounds and experiences. The collective intelligence of the "supermind" trumps individual brilliance repeatedly.[4] And therein lies the key to constructive disruption: Understanding that no one does it alone. By pairing human insights with tech-driven analysis, we can de-code the future.

Lay Groundwork for Future Change

What truly makes disruption constructive is when it benefits others who may not have a voice. It is not about changing things for the sake of change, but to reimagine how everyone involved can emerge from transformation with mutually beneficial outcomes. Indeed, when new circumstances lead us to try what has never been tried, we often find ourselves wondering why we waited so long.

Working in tech in the 1980s and 1990s, I was used to being the only woman in the room. But I made a seat for myself at every table possible, until it was normal for me to be there. One male colleague commented on what a difference it had made to have a female member on their board. "Why didn't we do this 10 years ago?" he said. "We didn't know what we were missing." During the pandemic, businesses that once estimated a shift to remote work would take a year were able to find a way to make it work in weeks or even days.[5] The implications for work–life balance and opportunities for new talent are still evolving. We are capable of more than we think is possible. With courage and ingenuity, future generations can benefit from the changes we make today.

Beginning now, there is a chance to overhaul how we work and how our businesses operate. Companies that embrace creative solutions, harness the boom in technology advancements, and look out for the people at the core of their workforce are the ones positioned to survive and thrive as we step toward what is next. To move with confidence into the future, we need constructive disruption now.

Three Things to Know or Do About Transformational Change

1. Transformational leadership and change stems from constructive disruption. It is an innovative mindset and approach to embracing times of upheaval as opportunities to make bold systemic moves, with an eye toward long-term success and a human-centered culture.
2. To find the breakthroughs that lead to success, use technology and data to learn from the future, and employ the wisdom of groups to solve unseen problems and tap invisible potential.
3. Rather than short-term wins, focus on innovative changes that lay the groundwork for long-term growth, advancement, and resiliency. The courage and fortitude we show now will pay dividends for future generations.

Re-mastering the Art of Connection in a Virtual World: The Platform Is Not the Problem

By Adrienne Shoch

The COVID-19 pandemic thrust teams into physically isolated virtual connections. This shift from a 3D world, rich with human sensing and intelligence, severed team members' intuitive access to one another.

For leaders and facilitators, the message is clear, but the required actions differ. This essay speaks to both.

The solution to the connection void is counter-intuitive for many organizations. Rather than trying to compensate for disconnection by building more sophisticated technology platforms, the wise strategy is to empower the source of effective team connection, self-awareness, and skillful empathy. These capabilities are essential for leading transformational change.

Self-Awareness

Awareness is fundamental to fostering connection and requires the ability to know yourself (internal awareness) and others (external awareness). Awareness is the convergence of our internal state (internal feelings, perceptions, and emotions) with the external environment (external structures, feelings, perceptions, and emotions of others) that creates the basis for connection. Once we have connection, we can influence, lead, and transform.

Internal awareness determines how effectively we connect with others. As in face-to-face settings, the same simple practices enhance virtual meetings. The first step in developing self-awareness involves cultivating your internal state and body awareness. Knowing your internal state requires self-inquiry and the answer to three questions:

1. Am I focused or scattered? Noticing the pace and chaos of thoughts gives insight into the quality of thinking.
2. What am I feeling (in one or two words)? Labeling feelings and emotions releases us from the experience and provides guidance as to what needs to shift and refocus.
3. What is my body doing? Body scanning provides access to physical awareness, energy level, and tension.

Experiencing and understanding our body shape awakens us to what is happening with our internal state. Feeling your body posture (i.e. sitting upright or slouched, shoulders shrugged or relaxed) is an internal gauge informing us of our physical state and what is happening inside. Amy Cuddy illustrates the importance of two body postures contributing to physical state.[6]

High Power – (Head and chin up, shoulders back, heart space out)

This posture increases testosterone and dopamine enhancing confidence, focus, and pleasure, while decreasing cortisol, a stress inhibitor. A visual representation is a victory stance of an athlete winning a race or scoring a winning point. This high-energy posture fosters confidence and connection and should be our default posture when working virtually.

Low Power – (Head and chin down, shoulders inwardly rotated, slouched spine, heart space concave)

This posture decreases testosterone and dopamine, thereby reducing confidence, focus, and pleasure while increasing cortisol and stress. A visual representation is looking at your phone. To demonstrate . . . pick up your phone now, and look at it. Notice where your body is. Are your head and chin down, are shoulders inwardly rotated, is the spine slouched, and is heart space sunken? This is a threat or defensive posture used for protection. This shape hinders our ability to connect.

Internal awareness is how we connect with ourselves in order to connect with others. Experiencing our body shape awakens us to what is happening with our internal state.

External Awareness

Similar to internal awareness, there are self-inquiry practices used to "tune-in" to our external environment. External awareness also requires self-inquiry and the answer to three questions:

1. What do I see around me? Observing what you see in your physical environment provides the pause needed to shift attention from internal to external awareness.
2. What is happening around me? Perceiving what is happening is an interpretation. With inadequate visual information, there is not enough information to know what is happening with those around you (i.e. how people feel, what they are doing). Perceptions are assumptions and require testing.
3. How do I know what is happening with those around me? A reality check serves to validate perceptions and provides insight into the internal state of others as well as accessible engagement.

A group self-inquiry practice, or "presencing check-in," accelerates the opportunity for connection with a three-step process at the beginning of a virtual meeting:

1. Invite attendees to pause, breathe, and share a word or two describing how they feel in the chat.
2. Remind them of the meeting's purpose and thank them for their attention.
3. Invite them to let go of everything they brought with them that no longer serves them or a productive meeting.

Many of us are in back-to-back meetings. Meetings and days feel like they run together. Without breaks, the brain and body get tired and disoriented. Pausing to separate daily experiences reminds us to let go of what no longer serves us as we progress through each meeting and day.

When we do not intentionally end or begin meetings, we lose our ability to distinguish between them, they run together, and we get tired. "Zoom fatigue," as it is known, is exacerbated from the inability to intentionally reorient and transition from one event to another. The brain has limited resources; it is not designed to sustain uninterrupted focus without rest. Zoom fatigue is a primary disabler of connection.

You could say there is an ongoing battle between the brain and technology when it comes to connection. Micro-images of headshots are not easily deciphered, and more information is required to feel safe and connected. Different skills are required in the new art of virtual connection to pause, reorient, and transition.

You can think of the brain as a continuous filter for safety and connection. With insufficient information, the imagination leads to a powerful bias toward negativity, and a reality check is required. This information void is exaggerated by technology.

Skillful Empathy

The battle between the brain and technology is neutralized with intentional listening and language. Listening through a lens of empathy cultivates external awareness. Adopting positive expressions, such as "good to see you" or "thanks for being here," neutralizes the nervous system and enhances safety and listening, especially in difficult conversations.

Skillful empathy experienced in communication and awareness is foundational for connection. Intentional listening and language allow us to effectively connect. No better thought leaders have mastered this than Otto Scharmer of MIT and Kim Cameron of the University of Michigan.

Otto Scharmer created the Four Levels of Listening. Knowing what you are listening for is like looking through an optic scope that magnifies your focus on a target. You know what you have to adjust to connect. Let us explore how it works.

Level One: *Downloading* – Listening from a place you already know. A default, autopilot which serves to validate what is already known.

Level Two: *Factual* – Listening to what is inconsistent with what you know to be true. This experience triggers awareness and heightens attention.

Level Three: *Empathetic* – Listening from a place in which others are speaking. This is the access point of connection. Intentionally relating to someone from the perspective of their experience.

Level Four: *Generative* – Listening from a place of emerging possibility. This is the access point to innovation and possibility.[7]

Listening intentionally *AND* being heard is synergy, serving connection at the deepest level.

From the perspective of the brain, language can be a weapon and a threat. Our job is to ensure that the receiver of our words can hear them. Kim Cameron found in his research on extraordinary performance, the ratio of 5:1 positive to negative expressions is a baseline for extraordinary performance in high-performing teams and our source to connection.[8]

This is the formula that our own research and client work have found so effective. Communicating with a weighted positivity bias creates high degrees of safety, mitigates unwarranted reactions, and can diminish negativity bias. There are five categories of Expressive Connectors used to maintain a ratio of 5:1 positive to negative expressions:

1. *Acknowledgment* – Expressions serving to create an experience of respect and being seen.
2. *Appreciation* – Expressions that simply make us feel good and create an experience of being held up and noticed.
3. *Empathy* – Expressions conveying a sense of understanding, trust, and connection.
4. *Inquiry* – Expressions serving to expand curiosity and external awareness while inviting engagement.
5. *Positive Intention* – A position, more than expression, serving to keep us safe and mitigate negativity bias.

Expressive Connectors are essential to safety. Together with skillful empathy and self-awareness, we are led back to the path of connection. These tools restore agency and empowerment.

Three Things to Know or Do About Transformational Change

1. Platforms do not help or hinder connection, people do.
2. The body plays a strategic role in connection and self-awareness.
3. The source of deep connection comes from Self-awareness and Skillful Empathy.

Notes

1. William A. Schiemann, *FULFILLED! Critical Choices: Work, Home, Life* (Salisbury: Secant Publishing, 2016), 1–5, 217–218.
2. Joseph B. Fuller, Manjari Raman, Eva Sage-Gavin, and Kristen Hines, "Hidden Workers: Untapped Talent" (Paper, Published by Harvard Business School Project on Managing the Future of Work and Accenture, Boston, MA, September 2021). www.hbs.edu/managing-the-future-of-work/Documents/research/hiddenworkers09032021.pdf
3. www.aspeninstitute.org/programs/upskill-america/, [August 31, 2021].
4. Thomas W. Malone, *Superminds: The Surprising Power of People and Computers Thinking Together* (New York: Little, Brown and Company, 2018).
5. www.mckinsey.com/business-functions/strategy-and-corporate-finance/our-insights/how-covid-19-has-pushed-companies-over-the-technology-tipping-point-and-transformed-business-forever, [August 30, 2021]
6. www.youtube.com/watch?v=Ks-_Mh1QhMc, [September 10, 2021].
7. www.youtube.com/watch?v=eLfXpRkVZaI, [September 10, 2021].
8. https://positiveorgs.bus.umich.edu/wp-content/uploads/Glance-Leading-Positively.pdf, [September 10, 2021], 1.

Chapter 4

Teams

Combating Sugarcoating and Toxic Positivity in Your Culture

By Steve Fitzgerald

It is 6:30 pm on a Tuesday and our meeting is starting two hours late. I have been called in to discuss building a dynamic feedback culture with the CEO of an early-stage biotech firm.

> "I work hard on getting our culture right," she says, diving headlong into the discussion. "We care about each other, energy and motivation are high, I make sure we offer flexibility, and demand inclusion. People feel valued, turnover is low, and we are doubling in size every six months."
>
> "Great," I say, "so what's the problem?"
>
> She sighs, pauses . . . and it comes out in a rush, "We are just terrible at giving anything but glowing feedback. *Really* bad. When I dig into the root causes of our mistakes, it's almost always the case that someone in the chain knew there was something amiss and didn't speak up, their voice got stifled, or didn't want to hurt someone's feelings."
>
> "Our people seldom tell each other the things they need to hear in order to improve. I call it *toxic positivity* and it's at the heart of us failing to get to the truth and making bad decisions. Help me fix that."

I hear this frequently from executives. Sometimes the root cause is toxic positivity, more often it is a hierarchy, or fear-based culture, where "saving face" really matters. Regardless of the cause, thoughtful leaders understand that an organization requires direct and open dialogue in order to ensure a truth-based culture, necessary reflection, and decisions rooted in reality, not perception.

In *Good to Great*, Jim Collins' highly influential 2001 book, he noted that "All good-to-great companies began the process of finding a path to greatness by

DOI: 10.4324/9781003227137-8

confronting the brutal facts of their current reality."[1] Leaders across industries, including category busters like Cargill, Netflix, and Bridgewater Associates (where I was once the Chief Talent Officer), attribute much of their prosperity to the value of direct, honest, and factual discourse. At Bridgewater the operating mantra is "Meaningful work and meaningful relationships through radical truth and radical transparency,"[2] and the hedge fund rotates around a culture of daily dynamic feedback at all levels.

Let us return to our CEO. "Look, I get the benefits, I'm sold on that. However, I have a colleague who attempted this change in his company, and it became a mess of infighting and back-stabbing. How do I avoid that?"

The primary challenge in this transformation is within each of us, located at the base of our brains. An object resides there called the amygdala, which regulates emotional expression. It organizes with other complex systems and our life experiences to shape our reactions to stimuli. One of the most fundamental of these instincts is the "fight or flight" reaction to a perceived threat.

We do not get to opt out of these reactions, they are hardwired into us by life experience. In a sense, the amygdala "learns" what to do when activated by the individual's perception of threat. For example, very young children who are reared in hostile, aggressive environments are much more likely to develop "fight" responses when they perceive others as aggressing against them, than are children who are raised in non-aggressive environments.[3]

When we are confronted with things that generate fear, such as disappointing feedback that makes us wonder if we are diminished in the eyes of others, our body responds and prepares to fight or flee. Our ability to rationally accept and consider information goes out the window, at least for the moment, until our frontal cortex can kick in and regulate those emotions.[4]

Recall Maslow's hierarchy of needs. He established the understanding that when one's safety or security is at risk, it is difficult to progress to higher-order needs like belongingness. If we are constantly being told by those around us that we are flawed, it can get in the way of belongingness unless it is handled with nuance.

With these processes operating uniquely in everyone, the irony is that feedback done poorly can work to impair learning, not enhance it. Here are strategies to overcome these challenges to achieve a balanced positive feedback environment.

Acculturation: Know Thyself

Train all people, and especially managers, in how to deliver and receive feedback. Practice it from the first week with the organization. Ensure a level of sophistication in matching the message with how an individual best receives it. For many, it will be surprisingly more difficult to give constructive feedback than to receive it.

Ensure a fundamental understanding of the brain's reaction to difficult feedback and provide coping strategies. For example, at Bridgewater we taught "sitting above" the feedback, detaching oneself from one's emotional response. While some were able to do that in the moment, for most it came after a period of reflection. Ray Dalio, the founder of Bridgewater, captured this process in his principle, Pain + Reflection = Progress.[5] These practices implicitly gave the individual "permission" to process at the speed required for effective reflection.

Promote Belongingness

Belongingness to a family, a community, an organization, etc., anchors individuals to an entity larger than themselves and leads to receptivity to stories, rituals, and routines resulting to a deeper sense of commitment. Instill core values around empathy, humility, and an esprit de corps. We are *special* because we have come through the crucible *together*.

Focus on Strengths and Guardrails Against Weaknesses

There is an adage in bicycle racing: "Race your strength and train your weakness." In a feedback-rich culture, we all discover our blind spots and weaknesses. Once people accept the reality that few of us are good at everything, this realization can be liberating.

- Match people to roles based on their strengths
- Oftentimes, our biggest blind spots reside in the shadow behind our towering strengths. For example, a data-centric analytical savant who cannot "read the room" during a board presentation. Create awareness of this reality
- If a leader has a known weakness, guardrail them with someone on their team who mitigates it

Control for Rater Error

Most of us are poor raters of the performance of others, so efforts must be made to correct the multitude of rater errors that happen in high-feedback cultures. At a minimum, a robust and frequent 360-degree rating system is needed, with training in controlling for bias of all sorts.

Bridgewater goes to another level with a proprietary system of daily behavior-based feedback, with the presumption that the patterns in the data will show the true tendencies of a person and the errors will be revealed as outliers.

Fine-Tune Based on Context

These changes can be difficult for independent-minded national cultures such as the USA, where many value the quality of ideas over age, hierarchy, or status. In other cultures, where deference to age, hierarchy, or other social norms are more dominant, frank feedback can be difficult for people because they are swimming against the current of their national culture. During rollout, adjust expectations and norms accordingly and evolve outliers back to a companywide norm over time.

Reflective feedback will improve anyone's critical thinking. That said, the organizational commitment to instilling it may vary by the likely impact on outcomes. Does the contract security guard or the receptionist need to be as deeply ingrained as your software developer leads? Is the solution the same for a fast-food company versus a hedge fund?

Selection

Back to my reply to the CEO:

> "I've saved the most important one until the end. We know that adopting new behaviors is hard, so I advise finding people who are already predisposed to thrive in a dynamic feedback culture. There are personality tests that can help with this, and I use them."
>
> "Even better, I find life experience to be a great indicator. Look to hire people who have experienced and thrived in a feedback-rich culture. They are more likely to have developed resilient behaviors that match the dynamic feedback environment and have developed a growth mindset. I also look for people who have goals beyond the next job. Everyone thinks of athletes here, and I have been on the practice field with coaches like Nick Saban: they are not wrong. But do not stop there: Dancers and debate champions come to mind as well."

She nodded and we got to work.

Three Things to Know or Do About Transformational Change

1. Individual intrinsic reactions to feedback affect us all. Managing this across an organization is essential in a dynamic feedback environment.
2. Selecting people already conditioned to a dynamic feedback-rich environment is the most important key to success.
3. Directed acculturation, shared expectations, savvy managers, and shared esprit de corps complete the Rx for change.

Transformation Through Inclusion and Belonging

By Sophia Kristjansson

Today, diversity of talent is often top-of-mind for CEOs and business leaders who consider it a strategic imperative that drives transformational change, including creativity and innovation.[6] However, even with a laser focus on increasing diversity across organizations, evidence exists that simply hiring diverse talent will not guarantee business benefits for Underrepresented Ethnic Groups (UEGs) in companies.[7] Unfortunately, missing out on these important voices, perspectives, and ideas wastes strategic opportunities for companies and strongly disadvantages them in the marketplace.

Leaders increasingly wonder why their efforts to build a diverse workforce do not automatically position them for strategic success. Evidence of why can be found in the numbers. Mercer, the human resources consulting firm, reports that Caucasians comprise 64% of entry-level workers, and 85% of positions at the top, showing that minorities face a promotion gap.[8] Additional data from Mercer shows that 81% of organizations say they are improving Diversity, Equity, and Inclusion (DEI) practices, whereas only 42% have a documented multi-year DEI strategy.[9]

In my position as a DEI consultant to Fortune 500 companies, I conducted my own investigation into this issue and asked managers why DEI best practices alone do not automatically result in better retention, promotion, or leadership development of heterogeneous employees. This research surfaced a common theme: While seeking better opportunities for diverse employees, managers consistently felt they were failing because their women and minority employees did not land the positions they were seeking. These managers believed that they understood and put into practice their organization's best DEI initiatives, yet they continually fell short in retaining and developing diverse talent to the highest level.

To accomplish more robust engagement of UEGs in the workplace, organizational leaders are exploring inclusion practices to ensure all employees feel that they have a voice on their teams. Inclusion practices help employees recognize that they are esteemed members of a team because they experience both belonging and uniqueness in everyday interactions on their teams.[10, 11] This approach focuses in on managers' behaviors, such as their ability to enlist contributions of all team members, develop go-to relationships across a team, and share decision-making in building inclusion in work groups and teams.[12] Although an interplay takes place between manager and employee inclusive behaviors, an employee's experience of the organization's culture is largely dependent on their manager's personality and approach to leadership, development, and, ultimately, retention.

The following experiment I conducted with one organizational leader shows how she is attempting to overcome bias and promote a team environment that includes and values all employees.

A Team Experiment in Inclusive Leadership

Sarah (fictionalized name), a VP of Sales leading a diverse workforce in a Fortune 500 company, approached me about her challenge to retain diverse talent and build teams that embraced cognitive complexity and valued challenging conversations. We landed on a concept of inclusive leadership developed by Randel and colleagues (please refer to the Theoretical Model of Inclusive Leadership in the Appendix). It identifies key leadership behaviors that foster both belonging and uniqueness in teams.[13]

Sarah felt she was not able to best support her diverse team and their needs. She strongly values cognitive diversity and psychological safety for her teams. However, Sarah observed that her managers struggled to engage their diverse team members, and attrition numbers showed employees leaving because they did not believe they had a voice in her organization. She was motivated to foster change and saw an opportunity to further develop her division by stretching her team to learn and employ inclusive leadership skills. Sarah's hope, after this experiment, was to find evidence of better job performance, reduced turnover, and more creativity and innovation across the board.

Our Co-created Iterative Learning Process

Participants committed to actively engaging in a three-month learning journey in which they would co-create an iterative learning process. The experiment included a total of 45 employees: Sarah, four directors, seven managers, and 33 part-time or full-time participants.

Ultimately, each participant was responsible for identifying and actively practicing inclusive leadership skills until they felt they had become second nature. For example, one team exercise involved solving a hard problem in a fun way to (i) foster communication and (ii) create techniques to solve difficult conversations. The goals were to (i) equalize status across teams and (ii) foster cognitive complexity by showing team members it was psychologically safe to disagree. Team members also learned how to work through any challenging aspects of a conversation in order to arrive at a better conclusion.

I served as the team's coach during the three-month process and made tweaks along the way to streamline learning and effectiveness. I fed back to them what I was learning and challenged them to think of their application of inclusive leadership skills differently. I gave Sarah and the participants feed-forward tricks (no more than three at a time) to use in the follow-up exercise. Pre-exercise and post-exercise micro learnings were available for the team to read and discuss.

The process also included a pre-inclusion and post-inclusion behaviors survey developed at Cornell University to examine feelings of inclusion at the individual, team, and organizational levels. Alongside HR, Sarah and I identified mechanisms to evaluate creativity, job performance, and turnover rates based on data the organization had already collected. Moving forward, the intention is to incorporate inclusive leadership skills into leader competencies.

Key Learnings

1. Managers consistently reported wanting to work well with their colleagues. At the beginning of the experiment, they did not feel well prepared to have challenging conversations with their team members in order to solve difficult problems. This point of view evolved once all employees understood the importance of psychological safety in creating a foundation of trust and rapport with their fellow colleagues.
2. The more engaged all participants were in designing how they would define and use the inclusive leadership skills, the more they were willing to actively engage with us and the process of learning. The experiment was a co-created iterative learning process for everyone involved. In the end, it resulted in teams that reported feeling strongly bonded with their colleagues.
3. The most successful experiments are simple and focus on one aspect of inclusive leadership skills at a time. This prioritization helped participants identify strengths in themselves and others to enhance the communication process.

Following the experiment, the attrition rate started to diminish across Sarah's organization. Participants reported feeling a greater sense of inclusion across their teams, and managers were commended for their inclusion skills in upward reviews. Communication across the division is now stronger and employees engage in tough conversations with respect. Time is taken to incorporate different points of view. Transformation through inclusion and belonging is an evolution Sarah and her employees are excited to model for their company.

Three Things to Know or Do About Transformational Change

1. DEI best practices are important organizational branding, but developing inclusive leadership skills on teams can make a difference in an employee's daily experience at work.
2. Change can be challenging to accept, and using a co-created iterative learning approach helps the people engaged in change take ownership of it.
3. Look for early adopters to help build engagement, and understand that disengagement might be because an individual does not feel like he/she/they is/are part of the group.

Coaching for Transformation

By Lacey Leone McLaughlin

Leadership is an ongoing journey of transformation and change. In order to lead, adaptation is imperative to sustaining a successful team, culture, and results. Often, coaching is a tool to help leaders do just that. Coaching can help drive reflection, planning, action and accountability, and when combined with building new or refining existing skills, it reveals the needed steps for transformation.

I was recently called to work with a creative artist and new founder of a value-driven entertainment organization (as well as her leadership team) that was looking to change the world through the content they intended to produce. The leadership team was clear on the content they planned to create as well as the impact they wanted to have on the world, and they were historically very talented in content creation. However, it quickly became clear that the skills used in creating are different than the skills used in leading, and this new team would need support. The team had the ability to bring stories to life, they created content, managed the process, and delivered an amazing product. But, running and building a business to support their creative vision proved to be difficult.

My client, a historically creative individual, needed to transform and grow into a business leader while balancing the need to continue to be a creative leader as well. She needed to successfully lead a team and a business that produced value-driven work for the company. From this realization, we began our coaching work with the goal of taking this creative individual and transforming them into a business leader.

When this engagement kicked off, it started with three goals: 1) Gain an understanding of the current state of the business, prioritize issues that needed to be addressed, and establish clarity around what success would look like; 2) Define the skills that needed to be developed and reinforced; and 3) Build in expectations and accountability as the business moved forward.

As we began digging into the current state of the business and leadership, it became obvious that the leader was allowing her leadership team to function independently with competing priorities and/or goals. When I asked the leadership team to describe their top priorities, I was expecting two or three items to stand out. To my surprise, I was given two pages of goals without any alignment. When asked to stack-rank the top five priorities, each person provided goals focused on their team and department. When I asked about the overall business goals, the team could not answer. It was clear that these leaders were each running their own department (basically what they viewed as their own world) with little to no consideration of the holistic impact on the business.

The next step was to bring the group together to talk about what the organization would look like in three to five years and what would lead to sustainability. Then, we considered what was getting in the way of achieving that vision. Finally, we allowed for conversations around how and why team members would know if it all worked. What would they define as success and how would they measure it?

Once we established what we were working toward, it was time to define what skills were needed to ensure success. What capabilities would need to be developed that would enable the company and leadership team to move from where they were to where they wanted to be?

For each of the team leaders, this process required a deep dive into their leadership gaps as individuals, as department members, and as a leadership team. We examined what was getting in the way, and what they could do more of to achieve the overall company goals. We identified the skills needed to get there, and the leaders set very clear expectations, timelines, and behaviors. Expectations and success were defined, and accountabilities were set to ensure goals were met.

For the founding leader, the start of this transformation was exhausting and did not show a lot of early results. Change proved to be difficult, and substantially harder than purely putting good content into the world. With a new, clearly defined, understanding of where the company was and where she needed it to be, she was able to own the task of setting expectations of her team and holding them accountable. She had to commit to leaving her comfort zone and learning to lead, having challenging conversations, and making changes quickly. Change slowly began to happen.

The first observable win happened when hiring decisions became easier. The team stopped bringing people on because of gut feel and candidates' creative abilities and started looking more holistically at their belief in the vision of the company, alignment around the approach to reach that vision, and technical skills required to realize the vision. Not surprisingly, in retrospect, these changes resulted in hiring employees who stayed longer and cared more.

Another observable win was that real conversations were happening. When team members made decisions that were inconsistent with a goal, they were respectfully called out, questions were asked, and changes were made. The team was no longer afraid to ask the hard questions and really get to the "why" of a challenge. The level of authenticity had clearly increased.

The founding leader made the following observation herself, "For the first time, not only was the team doing brilliant creative work, they were aligned, collaborating, and delivering towards a common goal." Wins felt like they were being achieved by the team (not just the department) and everyone celebrated them. Marks that were missed no longer led to finger-pointing, but rather to corrective actions, collaboration, and problem-solving.

From a business perspective, the team was beginning to hit and/or beat their deadlines. They were operating at/or under budget, all while creating the quality of work envisioned by the founder. The team was not only putting great content into the world but also doing it faster and at a lower cost.

About six months after this work started, the founding leader and I were reflecting on lessons learned and how she would take these wins and apply them to organizational success:

1. When things feel like they are not working, they are not. I must address them quickly.
2. As the leader, if I do not require and lead the change, it is not going to happen on its own.
3. I need to be clear on the goals and move out on them. Even small steps forward are still progress.

When things feel like they are not working, they are not. Address them quickly and act fast. Time spent by the founding leader or leadership team trying to figure out if something was really off was a distraction and costly. If she or the team would have just started addressing the issues, they would have achieved progress faster. The amount of time and effort wasted cost real money.

The founding leader also realized that once she identified the problem, the change needed to start with her. It would not happen without her being clear around goals and holding the team accountable.

Transformational change is often not fast, it is incremental. Small, clear steps towards a larger defined goal led to real change and impact. However, there must be an openness and willingness to transform. Establishing a culture that encourages and welcomes transformational change starts at the top and must have buy-in from leadership teams on down.

Three Things to Know or Do About Transformational Change

1. Gain clarity and an understanding of the current state of the business related to goals and what success will look like.
2. Define the skills that need to be developed and reinforced.
3. Build in expectations and accountability, and when things are not working, address them quickly. Start with yourself, be clear on the goals and the incremental steps to achieve them.

Arts-Based Dialogue as a Catalyst for Transformational Change

By Linda Naiman

This essay describes how a historical example of arts-based dialogue served as a catalyst for transformation in a business at a crossroads. Dialogue is one of the essential leadership capacities for sensing and shaping the future. An arts-based dialogue draws upon visual and metaphorical thinking processes to foster a cohesive understanding that illuminates new insights, enabling decision-making and action. This approach is a non-traditional but highly effective strategy for leading a team through transformational change.

When I met the Ginger Group Collaborative in 2004, they were a growing network of organizational consultants and educators from across Canada. They were struggling with two questions. Did they want to continue to invest time and energy in creating a new business venture? And if they were to form a collaborative strategic alliance, how would they work together? The Ginger Group was interested in the ways people work together in complex human systems, whether in teams, across organizations, or in whole communities, through collaboration and capacity development.

The Ginger Group was interested in how I use art to stimulate creativity and enhance collaboration and wanted to participate in painting processes "to get out of their heads" and access different ways of learning, which could be applied to their work.

Kate McLaren, one of the three founding members, explained,

> We had this dilemma. Do we have the energy and vision to stay together or don't we? Is it time to get into business together? Do we want to create a business plan? Are we going to get real or not? We were at a turning point.

So, the group invited me to bring my collaborative painting methods to their retreat as a way to help them have conversations they were finding difficult.

Marilyn Hamilton, another team member, said,

> Because we only get together twice a year, trying to maintain the momentum and clarity about what we're doing is always a challenge. This particular occasion was a way for us to go beyond simply the words and create a picture of the story that was in the process of unfolding.[14]

Hamilton observed,

> One of the things Linda did at the very beginning of our session together was to set up a container where she asked each person to share what

brilliance they'd brought to the meeting. That was a real trigger to bring forth the best of who we were. In naming what brilliance we were bringing to our time together it set up the opportunity for us to engage in image-making representations of what we thought our intentions were.[15]

In setting the container, I also asked everyone to listen for the brilliance in what others bring to the conversation, to build on each other's ideas rather than shoot them down.

We used a Visual Dialogue activity as an icebreaker to get acquainted and to stimulate creativity. The objective is to have a conversation using abstract imagery rather than words. Pairs took turns making abstract images on paper, in response to each other, and thus had a conversation. Once completed, each person shared their experience and the meaning they saw in their painting.

We communicate on many levels that are beyond words, and painting the conversation, rather than speaking, deepens our listening. The imagery generated by these conversations also illustrated in a graphic way the dynamics of the relationship between the pairs and this process provided illuminating insights for the group. We went through several rounds of visual dialogues with different partners. Once we debriefed the dialogues, I asked everyone to walk around the room and describe what they saw in each other's pictures. What did these images say about collaboration? This sparked a more involved discussion about artistic processes, collaboration, and how the Ginger Group was evolving.

The following day I asked everyone to paint a response to two questions: "How do I see my world?" and "Where am I at?" Each person painted alone, for five minutes. The group then moved from painting to painting, talking about the symbols and images they had each created, and what they saw in one another's work. Several of these dialogues were quite moving.

McLaren said,

> One of the painted stories emerged unexpectedly. It came from a member who was coming through an intense period of self-reflection after a major struggle at an institution she had left behind. Few of us knew this story. She told us later that when she began, she had no sense of what to paint and that the image seemed to create itself. In the painting, she had climbed into a craggy chasm with no footholds. Climbing down felt frightening and risky, "In climbing down, I began to see that instead of a bottomless cavern, what lay beneath me was not an abyss but a well, with all that means about replenishment and resources; but I had to be willing to climb down to get to them."

McLaren further observed,

> Although she was still climbing upwards, she pictured herself in the light above the purple depths, like a warrior queen who had discovered in the

unknown darkness a source of life. We had struck a vein of gold that helped us shape our future together.

The images revealed patterns, connections, and relationships that would never have been apparent otherwise. It is easier to talk about sensitive issues when you are referring to an image instead of each other. The painting processes helped set the tone for the structured discussion that followed. The images also helped the group to clarify their identity as a group and conveyed more powerfully than words what they had been trying to communicate.

In a second session, the group painted ten collaborative paintings. McLaren described her experience:

> In the end, each painting was a collective vision, yet each was very different! We created all these group visual stories that led us to a vision for ourselves. As we began to talk about our own shared creative experience, we could sense a deeper understanding beginning to emerge. We drew on the metaphors in the paintings to share observations and pose new questions about ourselves as individuals and as a collectivity. We were beginning to relax and "let it come."
>
> I think we appreciated later how big a turning point this was. We might not have had the commitment to keep trying to build this network by investing energy and personal financing if there hadn't been some kind of breakthrough or shift in our sense of purpose and identity. Painting got us out of our cognitive, explanatory, and analytical headspaces. It was an alternative form of expression. We didn't start with a narrative, but a story emerged from the process.

Another team member commented, "The paintings were a source of intimacy the group needs to stay together, and provided a forum for rich and insightful dialogue."

These painting exercises brought myths, symbolism, metaphors, and archetypes into the group's awareness, which helped everyone look at the journey it was taking. The process provided context for sensing and shaping the future they wanted to create as a new business enterprise.

McLaren concluded,

> We realized that the archetypes that emerged in the images of our painting represented the essence of what we wanted to convey about collaboration to our public. We have learned that it's not about making art, not about performance. It's about creating meaning together, using powerful visual symbols and images that come from the deepest parts of our being.[16]

One of the Ginger Group members summed it up, "It appears the human species has a way to communicate through picture storytelling that's very, very powerful. Storytelling is a powerful way of changing the world!"

Three Things to Know or Do About Transformational Change

1. Arts-based dialogue can be used as a discovery method for creating a desired future in organizations. The images created can help leaders effectively mediate complexity, discuss the undiscussable, evoke story-telling, and engage the hearts and minds of participants to explore new possibilities.
2. Art is an invitation to have a conversation. It is not about performance; it is about artful reflection and storytelling that helps us explore the landscape of complex issues.
3. Harness the power of art as a catalyst for transformation (at a personal, team, and organizational level) to make meaning out of chaos and uncertainty, imagine a better future, and tell a better story that moves people forward.

Notes

1. Jim Collins, *Good to Great* (New York: HarperCollins, 2001), 88.
2. Author's personal experience as CTO of Bridgewater Associates and Ray Dalio, *Principles* (New York: Simon and Schuster, 2017), 134–138.
3. Dr. Hi Fitzgerald, (University Distinguished Professor Emeritus, Developmental and Neurological Psychology, Michigan State University), in discussion with the author, July 2021.
4. Joseph LeDoux, *Anxious: Using the Brain to Understand and Treat Fear and Anxiety* (New York: Viking, 2015). Also see the Emotional Brain Institute (www.cns.nyu.edu/ebi/).
5. Dalio, *Principles*, 152–155.
6. Boris Groysberg and Katherine Connolly, "Great Leaders Who Make the Mix Work," *Harvard Business Review*, September 2013, 68–76.
7. Alison Cook and Christy Glass, "Above the Glass Ceiling: When are Women and Racial/Ethnic Minorities Promoted to CEO," *Strategic Management Journal* 35, no. 7 (June 2013): 1080–1089.
8. Pippa Stevens, www.cnbc.com/2020/06/11/companies-are-making-bold-prom-ises-about-greater-diversity-theres-a-long-way-to-go.html, [September 14, 2021].
9. Rayna Edwards, Rick Guzzo, Carole Jackson, Alex Knoepflmacher, and Haig Nal-bantian, *Let's Get Real About Equality: When Women Thrive 2020 DACH (Germany, Austria, Switzerland) Report* (Davos: Mercer, 2020).
10. Amy Randel, Benjamin Galvin, Lynn Shore, Karen Holcombe Ehrhart, Beth Chung, Michelle Dean, and Uma Kedharnath, "Inclusive Leadership: Realizing Positive Outcomes Through Belongingness and Being Valued for Uniqueness," *Human Resource Management Review* 28, no. 2 (June 2018): 190–203.
11. Lynn Shore, Amy Randel, Beth Chung, Michelle Dean, Karen Holcombe Ehrhart, and Gangaram Singh, "Inclusion and Diversity in Work Groups: A Review and Model for Future Research," *Journal of Management* 37, no. 4 (July 2011): 1262–1289.

12. Kenna Cottrill, Patricia Denise Lopez, and Calvin Hoffman, "How Authentic Leadership and Inclusion Benefit Organizations," *Equality, Diversity and Inclusion: An International Journal* 33, no. 3 (March 2014): 275–292.

13. David Mayer, Lisa Nishii, Benjamin Schneider, and Harold Goldstein, "The Precursors and Products of Justice Climates: Group Leader Antecedents and Employee Attitudinal Consequences," *Personnel Psychology* 60, no. 4 (November 2007): 929–963.

14. Susan M. Osborn, Ph.D., *Wake Me Up When the Data Is Over: How Organizations Use Stories to Drive Results*. (San Francisco: Jossey-Bass, a Wiley Imprint, 2006), 38–39.

15. Kate McLaren, "Finding a Vein of Gold through Painting a Story," *Storytelling Magazine* (May–June 2006): 20.

16. McLaren, "Finding a Vein of Gold through Painting a Story," 20.

Chapter 5

Organizations

Transformation Through Work Without Jobs

By Dr. John Boudreau and Jonathan Donner

Transformational change will increasingly happen with a new "work operating system," where tasks/projects are assigned to employees or machines or non-employees in talent marketplaces, where workers will be identified not as job holders, but through their full array of skills and talents.[1]

This new way of designing work and organizing talent requires leaders to think of transformational change through tasks and projects, not how "jobs" are organized and reorganized.[2] Transformational leaders must orchestrate a broad array of resources – some human, some not; some employees, some not – to execute those projects and tasks. When talent can choose projects and project leaders, transformational managers and workers will have a less hierarchical relationship.

Big Changes in the Role of Leaders

Top leaders often face this dilemma:

> I used to have people in boxes called jobs with reporting lines that ran to my box. Now, this new work operating system dissolves the boxes. "My people" are visible to other leaders through their capabilities, and other leaders can recruit "my people" for deconstructed tasks or projects. Who can I call on to get things done?

Large-scale transformation always transforms work, but it typically retains the job-based system, including reporting lines and employment. Yet, organizational transformation requires increased agility that will be impossible in this

DOI: 10.4324/9781003227137-9

slow-changing, job-based system. Organizational transformation increasingly demands that work be unfrozen from jobs, and a system capable of reinventing and assigning work without formal job descriptions. This demands different capabilities from leaders.

C-suite leaders will still set the strategic mission of the organization and define standards, goals, conditions, and resources that drive transformation. Functional leaders will still establish systems to align and support mid-level leaders, who prioritize and translate transformational goals into strategic objectives. Front-line managers will still define and prioritize the processes and tasks required to meet these objectives.

However, everyone will have additional vital roles in the new work operating system.

High-level functional leaders must now set broad guardrails that define how work is both delineated and coordinated across functions. Functions such as Finance, Operations, Facilities, Legal, Medical, HR, and IT must establish boundaries and principles about how work is accomplished, coordinated, and shared. Currently, those guardrails are set using jobs: New employees are assigned access to IT systems, clearances to handle sensitive materials, or the rights to enter certain facilities. But as jobs are deconstructed into sets of capabilities or tasks, which can be done by a wider variety of people including non-employees, setting and adapting these guardrails will have to be done quickly and continually, and will require rapid cross-functional coordination.

Transformational leaders must define the work and how it is accomplished and shared, but now through fluid tasks/projects and capabilities, not through jobs and hierarchy. Transformation strategies must now build an accepted framework for sharing and distributing power and accountability that must evolve in step with fluid work tools like internal talent marketplaces. This is key to avoiding chaos and ensuring that the new work operating system remains consistent with the strategy, purpose, and culture that define the transformation.

Front-line leaders will see the greatest change. They will still organize and optimize the goals of their units and the needs and desires of their workers, *but now in the currency of tasks/projects, and worker skills/capabilities.* They must become project leaders who perpetually deconstruct projects into tasks, and assemble workers into teams that optimize their deconstructed capabilities. Workers will typically no longer be exclusively assigned to a leader through a stable job hierarchy. When organizations adopt "work without jobs," the work and workers will be more free-floating, and leaders and managers will quickly assemble and disassemble teams to achieve the broader unit and organizational goals.

There will be fewer places for leaders to hide, and more opportunities to be seen. Leaders and managers will be defined less by title and credentials and more by achievements and character.

Transitioning to the New Work Operating System

So, transformation in the new work operating system requires strengthening and adapting traditional leadership skills and building new ones. Here are some examples.

From Process Execution to Project Guidance: Organizational transformation will increasingly happen through ongoing and evolving projects, rather than defined processes. Managers will source talent within and beyond the traditional organization, and rapidly assemble teams based on required skills and capabilities. Workers will increasingly connect with projects virtually through technology, so this evolved project management will more prominently reflect automation, distance collaboration, and influence. Traditional transformations might align using fixed transformation plans, but the new system will require real-time and perpetual coordination. Transformational leaders will apply tools much like those now used by agile teams (scrums, sprints, hacks, etc.).

From Hierarchical Authority to Empowerment and Alignment: Hierarchical authority will be less prominent in transformations using the new system of work without jobs, because workers will not be as tied to traditional reporting structures, and project-based work requires teams to increasingly self-manage. The transparent new system will make work opportunities visible to workers through a continually updated array of options. Employees will demand work that meets their personal preferences and the freedom to shift between projects. Transformation leaders must set strong frameworks that balance worker empowerment with accountability that reflects the broader task/mission. They must discern when and how to negotiate, whether to negotiate formally or informally, and how to attain team and individual alignment about how value is created and shared.

From Technical to Humanistic Work Automation: Work automation will increasingly require work without jobs. Organizational transformation will encounter more frequent, and visible, choices between replacing, augmenting, and reinventing the human worker,[3] often by giving humans new and more valuable capabilities that are only possible through automation. Leaders may assume that automation always produces greater predictability and efficiency. But as such choices will increasingly occur at the project level, managers will need a more nuanced understanding of what humans can contribute in aesthetic creativity, cultural perspective, and innovative potential.

From Episodic to Continual Focus on Diversity, Equity, and Inclusion (DEI): The traditional job-based system inclines leaders to consider DEI episodically, when hiring or promoting. Yet, it is ongoing relationships and interactions that more often determine DEI. Transformation through a system of work without jobs presents far more frequent opportunities to choose, assign, reward, and develop team members, as tasks/projects and team memberships are perpetually reinvented. This approach could significantly enhance DEI efforts through more opportunities. Yet, if bias persists, this issue could simply produce more and faster non-inclusive choices. Transformational leaders must create processes for continually assessing whether work, and its remuneration, are distributed equitably.

From Results–Based to Purpose–Led: The foundational pillar is purpose-led work. This is the key question: "Why should anyone be led by you?"[4] This question becomes even more important as human talent gains agency and autonomy to choose work, in service of serial teams and multiple leaders. To continually and successfully assemble teams in the new work operating system, transformational leaders must nurture a more transparent leadership brand. This brand will be revealed by leaders' past projects, and embodied in marketplace ratings by former team members: How much can you learn by working with this leader? How open and flexible are they to innovation and different styles of work and contribution? The new system may embody a perpetually updated Leader Net Promoter Score (NPS), the percentage of promoters minus detractors based on the question "How likely are you to recommend this leader to a friend or colleague?"

As workers travel through fast-changing roles, working serially for many project managers, they will more quickly discern those leaders that share their aspirations for value beyond task success. The increased speed and granularity of work will prize leaders whose purpose is like the keel of a sailboat, steadying and guiding it toward a destination even as it tacks through shifting winds.

Three Things to Know or Do About Transformational Change

This new, *agile, serial leadership* will require leaders/managers to build all transformations on:

1. Defining, tracking, and increasing accountability for purpose-driven leadership.
2. Deconstructing jobs and adopting the fundamental unit of transformation as transient and highly efficient teams.
3. Blending (not replacing) humans and work automation technology.

Global HR Organization Transformation

By Maria Forbes

Transforming how a global function operates needs alignment and constant engagement. When you are introducing a new way of operating you will spend more time convincing than expected (even when your audience is senior HR leaders who are well versed in transformative change). You will also need to ensure function leaders and influencers take ownership, to shape and drive change.

This example of transformational change sits within the Global HR function of one of the largest Food and Beverage organizations in the world. Its HR leaders operate in diverse markets and categories that have unique, but familiar needs.

The Board of this organization challenged HR to come in line with the organization's transformation goals, to drive improved results and reduce overheads, while still delivering better service offerings to their global and local businesses. As a senior HR Director, Christopher was leading efforts to drive transformation throughout the Global HR Talent organization and co-leading the HR organization transformation. The success of this transformation was influenced by the approach he adopted to engage the HR leader network and the introduction of a community mindset concept to strengthen the HR service offering to the business.

Establishing the Rationale for Change

Christopher ignited a collaborative approach to building the future together, with HR leaders and influencers coming together as a global community to shape talent processes. The focus was to streamline and deliver consistent standards and experiences across the globe. Change included introducing the hot topic of the future of work and included new capabilities within HR to deliver needed transformation.

The HR leadership team came together to build common core processes and identify priorities, accompanied by the Board's desire to improve the business in every function. The rationale for the change was clearly understood:

- The HR global community needed to consider itself as a competitive advantage to the organization regardless of the different markets they operated in.
- HR needed to provide access to the best talent, capability, and tools across the globe.

- HR was required to deliver upgraded talent through stronger leader development solutions.
- HR's goal included having each business leader in all markets benefit from the same set of high-standard solutions.

Involving Leaders in Design

Critical to success was having HR leaders and influencers heavily involved in building global processes; implementing the change and "living the change" would set the stage for delivering as a community.

Christopher engaged the HR leader community in the core process called "Hire to Retire." In a series of workshop settings, he generated dialogue among leaders, bringing their own market perspectives and introducing them to a framework identifying talent processes they needed to address. Up to 30 new sub-processes were identified and prioritized using a grid to position the "frequency of use" and "level of expertise" in their markets.

Christopher also introduced the concept of *subsidiarity* – the notion that in early communities people are organized around those best capable for a task, which gives strength to the whole community. Christopher's interpretation of subsidiarity in the context of this HR organization transformation was the notion that if it can be done better (more simply in a smaller decentralized, market, wherever the market is located), it would better serve the whole community.

The HR organization already had a well-established practice of shared service centers. However, this transformational change was about capability excellence accessed in a different way than traditional centralized services. There were varying levels of team maturity across significantly diverse markets, and duplication was caused by larger organizations designating capabilities for their own respective markets.

The HR team agreed to initially focus on the key challenge of talent sourcing. Only three markets had these capabilities and expertise while the others were short of skills and at infancy stage. A strategy was agreed upon, where the three markets would lead, and others would build and learn from them and share capabilities.

Christopher reminded us that we must all have the courage and humility to see people who can do it better than ourselves. His approach fit comfortably with the organization's goals to simplify, standardize, and share.

Another critical component of this transformation was to have HR leaders both own and actively shape the design of the change, thereby aligning closely with the challenge parameters and goals set by the Board. The major challenge for the HR leaders was to give up appealing activities and local expertise that they had previously fully controlled. In addition, these HR leaders had to explain to the business why they were relinquishing local market expertise and control to other markets.

A Strong Emphasis on Convincing

There were three main stakeholders in the process that had to be convinced to take forward a plan for large-scale transformation:

1. **Senior HR community leaders** who were most concerned with losing control of value-added activities in their local markets and the resulting potential exodus of talented individuals.
2. **The Executive Board and business leaders** who were now being asked by HR to build new expert teams, which seemed contrary to the organization's goal of reducing size.
3. **HR specialists** who were asked to support the change, move to a new organization model that did not previously exist, and take the risk to leave secure jobs to join a new internal boutique consulting organization.

This convincing stage took considerable time before further progress could be made. It started with a vision and continued with evangelizing and building a team to design the change.

To convince HR, the focus had to be on specific activities that the local market organizations would be willing to recognize and benefit from, particularly those capabilities they were not in the best position to currently deliver. This was a helpful focus during the process of change.

To successfully carry out the transformation, HR would have to invest in technology, enabling HR to be more efficient in terms of reducing heads, decreasing dependency on external services, and minimizing duplication of costs across markets. Initially, the project approach was set for a "big bang" delivery. Through the convincing stage, it became clear that a step-by-step approach was more appropriate and would allow the team to close a chapter if something did not work.

Finally, the execution of this initiative also needed to be in a phased approach. It would allow for proof points to address concerns of the Executive Board, so that they were not signing a blank check without evidence of success.

Resistance to Change

The greatest resistance to this transformation was initially from the Executive Board, where it took several attempts to secure their buy-in. Finding the right language that was meaningful to the Board was critical. The greatest selling opportunity was within the field of proactive talent sourcing, which was new to the organization and where HR used language that was not easily understood by the business. Christopher and his team had to avoid typical HR language and adopt more business-specific terminology. Without convincing the Board, they could not move forward with such a major shift in the operating model.

Resistance also came from within HR leader and director communities. The vision and design detail on how this new approach would work were accepted. However, when the new way of operating began, resistance started, due mainly to the concern that people were losing local control. It became much more difficult at this point in the transformational change journey.

Christopher stressed that plans must, at all times, remain flexible and agile and implemented with a degree of bravery.

When Christopher presented his plans to the Board, the Board member who had previously been the most vocal opponent of the proposed changes, expressed his respect for the courage it took to change the plan, and for the realism required to recognize the change needed. Christopher and the HR leader team were given the green light to deliver improved HR professional services across the global organization, maximizing the best capabilities, both globally and locally.

Three Things to Know or Do About Transformational Change

1. Involve market leaders and influencers in the transformation design and identification of priority areas. Their perspectives will ensure that what you are doing will realize the benefits across the organization.
2. Be prepared when transformation shifts to the implementation phase, when personal loss surfaces and execution commitment can be undermined. Ensure all stakeholders are convinced of the concept and of the need to execute.
3. When introducing a new way of operating, lead with *Agility, Sensemaking, and Bravery.* Do not be too rigid, you will have more credibility and success when you adapt as you learn.

Transformation Through Adaptive Leadership

By Lori Heffelfinger and Sally Breyley Parker

Leaders and organizations are dealing with unprecedented change and disruption driven by increasing complexity. To survive and thrive in this climate, business and HR leaders must Lead Adaptively. This essay discusses both Adaptive Organizations and the Adaptive Leadership required to lead those organizations using the Four Practices of an Adaptive Leader: 1) Diagnosing *then* Acting, 2) Navigating and Tackling Adaptive Challenges, 3) Valuing Diversity, and 4) Embracing Discomfort.

Adaptive Organizations

The past two years have illuminated one key lesson: **organizations that want to survive and thrive must be able to continuously and effectively adapt in an environment that is increasingly Volatile, Uncertain, Complex, and Ambiguous (VUCA).**

As the sand continues to shift beneath their feet, leaders find the past to be a less reliable guide for action. By "the past," we can be talking about the last ten years, one year, even one month. Just look at how strategic priorities have shifted in one year. For instance, a 2020 survey by Boston University and Future Workplace highlighted employee experience, leadership development, learning transformation, next-generation leaders, and people analytics as top priorities. But in 2021, those priorities shifted to employee well-being/mental health, followed by DEI, leadership development, employee experience, and managing remote workers.[5]

The fact is, we **live in a state of dynamic non-equilibrium** where organisms, ecosystems, and organizations alike are operating in a constant state of flux. Conditions (both internal and external) are never quite the same from day to day. The changes we face are NOT moving us toward some "new state" of stability, order, or predictability. Plus, the speed of change requires organizations to adapt in shorter time cycles and increasingly sophisticated ways because our environment and our ecosystems are increasingly complex and ever changing.

To thrive in this environment, organizations need to re-perceive change, shifting the perspective from an event to be managed on a path to a new status quo, to a core capability of business evolution.

Adaptive Leadership

Adaptive Organizations also require Adaptive Leaders who engage in mobilizing people to tackle tough challenges and thrive. There are four practices in which Adaptive Leaders must engage.

Diagnosing Then Acting
Slowing Down to Speed Up

There is pressure to move into action quickly in most organizations, often without collecting sufficient data and exploring possible interpretations and interventions. But with adaptive challenges, diagnosis is the most critical skill. Unfortunately, it is also the most undervalued. Leaders have been socialized and trained to be good at action, solve problems decisively, and have answers. There is often little incentive for diagnosing the larger picture when "people who look to you for solutions have a stake in keeping you focused on what is right in front of your eyes."[6]

Adaptive Leadership requires two levels of diagnosis and action: the organization system and the self. In other words, a leader needs perspective on their complex organizational context (history, patterns, culture) and themselves (attitudes, behaviors, habits). Leading adaptively also requires both an ability to attend to events around you *and* an ability to see the broader patterns and dynamics playing out.

Navigating and Tackling Adaptive Challenges
The People With the Challenge Take on the Challenge

Leaders need to recognize that today's challenges are **"Adaptive Challenges," which are difficult to identify and easy to deny because the challenge is an inherent aspect of the larger whole.** (Example: Hybrid Work affects not just the employee requesting it, but their team, their department, the larger organization, and even customers and suppliers, and the implications of it could vary significantly across organizations and regions. Therefore, most organizations are struggling with whether to implement Hybrid Work or not, and how to do it).

Rather than bringing in an expert, the people with the challenge need to address it. Many if not most of these challenges require working across organizational boundaries. Crossing boundaries adds to the complexity and requires leaders to work outside their functional and direct lines of control. It requires them to influence, collaborate, and navigate decision-making across diverse sets of stakeholders.

> **Adaptive Challenges can only be addressed by changing people's priorities, beliefs, habits, and loyalties. Making progress requires going beyond any authoritative expertise to mobilize discovery, shedding certain entrenched ways, tolerating losses, and generating new capacity to thrive anew.**[7]

It is easier to solve a "technical problem" – instituting a policy or assigning the problem to the managers to solve on their own – than to accept an "Adaptive Challenge" – looking at the larger organization as a whole and the entire design-build process involving all the key stakeholders along the design path.

Valuing Diversity and Engaging Diverse Views

Akin to understanding Adaptive Challenges is the ability to value and engage diverse views. In fact, it is essential to solving Adaptive Challenges.

No one person or team can possibly have all the answers. All share responsibility for the organization's future. Everyone must play their part, and this means creating a culture and space for differing views, which may be hard to do, given the complexity and polarities of perspectives existing in the workplace and our communities.

Engaging the diversity of views in an organization amplifies its inner voice. Unlike the voices of individuals that often seek to maintain self-interest, **the inner voice of the organization** speaks in service to the whole of the organization. This voice is powerful because it

> bows to truth and pays little homage to power. It seeks to expose painful realities. In seeking the collective good, the inner voice does not distort the need for sacrifice and change by deferring to the preferences of a particular individual. The inner voice of the organization is often a threat to those in authority.[8]

Adaptive Leadership takes immense courage and conviction to see the whole, to see systems, to see what others might not see from their various vantage points, to be open to the unknown, to tap the wisdom beyond one's experience, and perhaps even comprehension. In essence, to be vulnerable.

Leaders must rely on others to share their perspectives. Leaders also must bring their perspectives, which may at times be different from the others. They must risk conflict, knowing that it is in service of a larger purpose, the organization's purpose.

The open expression of divergent perspectives will, in the end, yield a better outcome.

Embracing Discomfort
The Space for Learning

Transformational change or **real change** requires what Robert Quinn calls **"Deep Change," new ways of thinking and being**. An organization only changes when the people move it to change, but this **requires those individuals to dig deep within themselves to find that capacity to change.** This change requires continuous learning, self-reflection, and the desire to change no matter how hard it is.

The good news about digging deep to do this hard work as a leader is that **it models how others can do their hard work**. It also prevents employee burnout.

When an organization is in "collective denial" about the need to change, the organization is on the "Road of Slow Death." Everyone knows the organization needs to change. Still, no one talks about it, and everyone keeps working, keeps busy, and thinking as always, but they begin to burn out in the process. This individual burnout leads to collective burnout or demise. Overcoming this collective demise requires the ability to overcome denial.

Deep change requires **tapping our inner resources,** knowing what we are passionate about, what we fear, and what we resist. It requires owning our strengths and admitting our weaknesses, and most of all, asking for help.

Deep change requires new ways of thinking and being. It is significant in scope, discontinuous from the past, and usually irreversible. It distorts existing patterns of action and involves taking risks. It means surrendering control.

Most of us build our identity around our knowledge and competence in employing specific known techniques or abilities. Making deep change involves abandoning both, and "walking naked into the land of uncertainty."[9] This transformation can be a terrifying choice, a dark night of the soul. While making incremental improvements can be beneficial, reinvention requires deep change, at both the organizational and individual levels.

> **It is not change by itself that makes us uncomfortable; it is not even change that involves taking on something very difficult. Rather, it is change that leaves us feeling defenseless before the dangers we "know" to be present that causes us anxiety.**[10]

Three Things to Know or Do About Transformational Change

1. Diagnose and then act.
2. Value diversity and engage diverse views.
3. Embrace discomfort to learn and grow.

Leverage Change: If You Want to Transform Your Organization, Start by Changing Your Own Paradigms

By Robert "Jake" Jacobs and Susan Schmitt Winchester

Transforming organizations takes years, is hard work, and often leads to disappointing results. This is common wisdom. It has been proven time and again. It goes with the territory. But, it does not have to be that way.

Most approaches to transformational change are littered with flawed paradigms. Paradigms that inherently lead to these efforts falling short of the mark. Want different results? See the world in new ways.

Uncommon wisdom makes it possible to achieve faster, easier, better results with any transformation effort, in any organization, made by anyone. The approach we are describing is chockfull of new paradigms, fresh perspectives on problems that have plagued organizations for years. Welcome to the world of Leverage Change.

Leverage Change

Leverage Change[11] is a flexible approach to applying eight ways for individuals, teams, and organizations to transform faster, easier, and better than you believe possible. You can use it to turbocharge a change method you are already using or as the foundation for one you are developing. It applies equally well to simple efforts involving a few people to complex ones engaging tens of thousands. Benefit from it as you launch a transformation effort and reap rewards if your work is already underway. Be the "go to" person when it comes to change, advancing your career and organization alike.

Adopt the paradigm of leverage and accomplish more with fewer hassles, headaches, and problems. Archimedes, a third century BC Greek mathematician, described the power of leverage when he said, "Give me a lever long enough, and a fulcrum on which to place it, and single-handed I shall move the world." You can move your worlds in the arena of transformation by changing your paradigms about how it happens. Leverage Change is your guide map along this journey.

Leverage Change is comprised of eight levers, or smart, strategic actions, that yield profound results. Each addresses a common problem that prevents transformation efforts from succeeding (see Table 5.1). While there are eight powerful ways available in creating effective transformations, we are going to focus on one that addresses a frequent frustration of leaders: change taking too long.

Organizations pay a steep price for slow transformation efforts, even when they can eventually claim victory from their work. While you are toiling away, competition is winning new markets, commercializing leading-edge

Table 5.1 Common Problems With Transformation Work and Levers That Address Them.

Common Problem	Lever That Addresses It
There is too much change	Pay Attention to Continuity
Change takes too long	Think and Act as If the Future Were Now!
People reject your change approach because it is "Not Invented Here"	Design It Yourself
People do not know enough to make good decisions	Create a Common Database
All change efforts must begin from the top	Start with Impact, Follow the Energy
So many ask "What is in it for me?"	Develop a Future People Want to Call Their Own
People get to do only the routine work of their regular job	Find Opportunities for People to Make a Meaningful Difference
People's plates are already full	Make Change Work Part of Daily Work

technologies, making valuable process improvements, and creating cultures that lead to advantages in the recruitment and retention of top talent.

Living in a Leverage Change World

How can you reduce the time it takes to transform an organization from years to months? Embrace a new paradigm, the lever noted above called Think and Act as if the Future Were Now! Instead of seeing the future as something "out there" that will occur at a later point in time, choose to live it today. Here. Now. When you and your entire organization make this shift, transformation occurs rapidly, even in some cases instantaneously.

Your old paradigm told you that transforming culture takes years. Plenty of experts will tell you the same. Do not buy it. Your new culture will take years to create because you believe it will. If you want a more participative culture, think and act as if this close collaboration already exists. This paradigm shift immediately changes the game. In this new reality, who should be in the room for your next meeting? What criteria should you be using to make decisions today? How much power should different stakeholders hold right now? Stop talking about the future. Start living it.

Then encourage others to join you in this journey. Create an organization that subscribes to this new paradigm. Benefits of effective change work accrue to the bold. Colleagues previously reticent to jump aboard the transformation train see and hear change occurring all around them. Their belief that this time it is for real increases significantly. As they begin thinking and acting as if the future were now, their colleagues' faith in the future being real creates a virtuous cycle of ongoing transformation. At the same time, you will be collecting financial, quality, customer satisfaction, and other "winnings" sooner and will be able to reinvest them, further stoking the engine of your transformation efforts.

A Transformation Challenge

Susan has written a book called *Healing at Work*.[12] It is about how to use career conflicts to overcome your past and build the future you deserve. It is based on research she and her co-author Martha Finney have done with what they call Adult Survivors of Damaged Pasts (ASDPs). ASDPs have experienced some type of trauma growing up. In fact, nearly two-third of adults have suffered at least one of 10 adverse childhood experiences.[13] This trauma often leads to one being an overachiever who never rests to enjoy successes, does not believe they ever do enough, becoming people pleasers or bullies, to name a few characteristics. Organizations are filled with these people. You may even be one of them yourself. This terrible burden is not borne only by the ASDPs.

Organizational costs of burnout, reduced performance, toxic cultures, health-related problems, addictions, and ineffective teams all result from not addressing this issue. Transforming your culture to be a healthy, vibrant, supportive place for ASDPs (and everyone else) is a tough task when the work you are doing needs to be deep enough to include these issues.

How does the lever Think and Act as if the Future Were Now! accelerate transforming a culture where ASDPs thrive and contribute their full potential? We outline how to do this, providing answers to our culture transformation effort as examples. Pick your own transformation work (for yourself, your team, or your organization) and respond to each of the steps for your own benefit.

Paradigms help us make sense of our organizations. They can also get in the way. Change your paradigms. Transform your organization.

Three Things to Know or Do About Transformational Change

1. Describe the essential elements of the preferred future you aspire to create. An environment where time spent having negative, emotional over-reactions to another, often fueled by old scripts and self-limiting beliefs, is minimized. When workplace conflicts occur, we have in-the-moment interpretations leading to healthier reactions, decisions, and actions.

2. If you were already living in this preferred future, how would you be thinking and what actions would you be taking right now?

   a. See the workplace as a laboratory for emotional healing rather than a place of stress and friction.

   b. Model for my team how to take "time outs" during heated conflicts.

   c. Check if my thinking is distorted such as "When my boss is in a bad mood, it must have been something I have done."

   d. Ask myself, "Am I sure? Is this true?"

   e. Rationally assess how I respond to conflict and if and how my past experiences are influencing my present choices.

   f. Share what I am learning about myself with my team.

3. Invite others to join you in Thinking and Acting as if the Future Were Now! I will invite my direct reports at my next team meeting to partner with me in taking active steps to practice responding when we get emotionally triggered at work, resulting in less stress.

Sustainable Diversity, Equity, and Inclusion (DEI): Transformational Change at the Individual, Team, and Organizational Levels

By Karen Jaw-Madson

The graveyard of dead DEI initiatives cannot deter the pursuit of more diverse, equitable, and inclusive organizations. Both the upsides of success and the consequences of inaction are too great. Failures in DEI are rooted in a variety of factors, but all share this in common; *they lack the sustainable results in time to make a difference.*

Sustainable results imply a degree of generative continuity, momentum is critical. In change management, the transformation has to stick for as long as it is needed, and arrive no sooner or last no longer. Results come in the form of discernable progress, not just milestones and metrics, but a shared belief that sufficient improvement has been achieved.

Time is as paradoxical in business as it is in life. Social inequity at work is not built overnight, and neither is equity. There have been many opportunities for course corrections along the way, but somehow the reckoning is sudden, and people and organizations are often unprepared. Yet, while there is a lot of regret for what has come too late, all is not lost. In most cases, there is still time to attain sustainable DEI with just-in-time results, starting now.

Underperformance in sustainable DEI begins with saturation problems. Without breadth and depth, there is not enough to drive the momentum for sustainability. For starters, many people and organizations fail to go beyond "initiatives." They treat DEI like another project, siloed or added on instead of the systemic, ongoing, and fundamental change it has to be.

Culture, for example, is arguably the foundation of how a business operates. But, it is often a footnote in the DEI discourse, considered separately when DEI and culture should be interdependent. Implementing DEI without changing a culture to support it guarantees superficial outcomes.

Still, that is not enough. Not only is there more to align throughout the entire system, but changing a culture to be more diverse, equitable, and inclusive requires penetration at all levels – individually, on teams, and organizationally. This comprehensive approach may sound intimidating, but we are equipped to rise to this challenge. The following actions are just some of the many possible ways that illustrate just how accessible sustainable transformational change in DEI can be if an organization is willing to grasp it.

Individuals

Most people believe it is beyond their ability to influence company culture. The reality is that with the right mindset, tools, and motivation, one person can indeed make a difference. For those who want to move from bystander to ally, granting that "permission" may be enough to inspire action.

Engage in personal transformation. This is done by combining self-awareness with continuous learning. Both activities build one's knowledge. Transformation comes from utilizing that knowledge. Answer the following questions:

- What are your values, needs, and motivations?
- How have they been shaped by experiences?
- What assumptions and biases must be overcome?
- What should be learned?
- What resources are available?
- What skills or talents can you leverage?
- What role(s) do you want to play in making your workplace more diverse, equitable, and inclusive?

Doing this work also helps you understand how you interact with others in your own context. Enhancing leadership skills like learning agility, empathy, cultural and emotional intelligence, and networking will equip an individual to be a better ally at work. Everyone can decide how they want to evolve as an ally, including you.

Demonstrate allyship by taking action. Perhaps the organization has identified behaviors to demonstrate diversity as a value. Allies should role model these ideals. In the absence of that, you can apply what you have learned and determine how you show allyship.

You can also identify and break unproductive behavioral patterns that erode DEI in day-to-day interactions, whether overtly or via microinequities. Disrupting those patterns forces others around you to respond differently. This can come in the form of standing up for oneself, advocating, or amplifying colleagues. Others will follow your lead. With enough consistency, new patterns are established, and culture changes over time.

Partner with others, because this is also one of the most important steps an individual can take. It can come in different forms, but the idea is to give and get support by building community, where people can combine superpowers for exponential effect. This strategy grows the solidarity dividend, what Heather McGhee defined as "gains that come when people come together across race, to accomplish what we simply can't do on our own."[14]

Teams

Teams are where the work of individuals, culture change, and DEI implementation begins to scale. It is within every team's power to manage their own culture and prove how they can leverage DEI.

Increase team awareness to uncover critical information on needs, motivations, strengths, blind spots, and opportunities that impact performance. Understanding the individuals on the team, how they collaborate, and how that aligns with their work not only supports talent optimization but also promotes an appreciation for their diversity. There are many tools available to do this, but maintaining that awareness is the true differentiator.

Establish and preserve psychological safety. This is a necessary condition for team performance, change, and DEI. Team members must believe that having differences not only is okay but encouraged because it leads to better outcomes. Research has shown that trust, respect, and care for one another are ingredients for psychological safety.[15] This is something all workers desire regardless of background but is especially needed for DEI.

Create a social contract that ensures DEI. Develop a team charter as a group to engage and align members. In addition to purpose, principles, and processes, determine:

- How do we engage each other and commit?
- How can we establish psychological safety and trust?
- What norms do we want to emphasize?
- How will we be role models of DEI?
- How will we manage conflict?
- How will we cultivate connection?
- How should we codify expected behaviors and carry them out with commitment and accountability?

Organizations

The ultimate goal is to deliver sustainable, organization-wide transformation. Having DEI as an enduring competitive advantage requires adoption into core values, systemic integration, and matching lived experiences. Design of Work Experience (DOWE), as explained in *Culture Your Culture: Innovating Experiences @ Work*, provides an in-depth understanding of the current state, a design for the future state, and a roadmap with action plans for how to get there.[16]

Get a baseline. This is the first, crucial step of DOWE. Building awareness at the organizational level calls for a deep understanding of the complexities of the current culture. The process of acquiring that knowledge engages people from the very beginning of the transformation journey and indicates what will most likely be successful given a company's unique context. Without that deep understanding, everything else is trial and error.

Co-create the DEI strategy to align with the culture and employee experience. There are no better collaborators than the people expected to carry out the vision for the future. In the Create & Learn, Decide, and Plan phases of DOWE, leadership and employees partner to design the strategy blueprint, roadmap, and action plans for adopting DEI holistically. This construct brings together and leverages the diversity of knowledge, talent, and experience across the organization.

Implement change with the guidance of the roadmap and action plans that are constructed through the DOWE process. Plans include the content of the change itself and "the how" of implementation. Both drive the momentum necessary for change.

Sustain on a continuous basis. This step determines success or failure based on how well desirable changes take hold. Meaningful substance and momentum must permeate at all levels. The benefits of change are realized as long as the organization continues to pay attention and manage it.

While there is more to discover, a body of knowledge exists around the nature of transformational change. There are answers; the challenge is in execution. Generating enough momentum, depth, and breadth will sustain change. People must always be engaged to drive it. Even with the best of intentions, organizations may still fall short. But, DEI is worthy of attempt after attempt, until it is achieved and sustained.

Three Things to Know or Do About Transformational Change

1. Engage people before, during, and after change.
2. DEI requires systemic changes, including in the culture.
3. Sustainable change can be achieved through momentum, depth, and breadth at the individual, team, and organizational levels.

Transformational Change and the Employee Lifecycle

By Heather Laychak

Given the myriad of economic, environmental, political, racial, and social disruptions that occurred during a global pandemic, I would be hard-pressed to find anyone on the planet who would disagree with Heraclitus who said, *"Change is the only constant."*

Countless transformational leadership experts have taught us that organizations that effectively lead and manage change are more successful. Organizational resilience and adaptability are competitive differentiators and there is no shortage of change management models or business cases to reference. So, why is managing change so hard and how do we get better at it?

Gary Hamel, an internationally recognized business strategist said, *"You can't build an adaptable organization without adaptable people – and individuals change only when they have to, or when they want to."*[17] Therein lies the challenge.

Throughout my career, I have faced numerous business and organizational challenges that required me to apply and provide change management leadership. I can distinctly recall the first real change effort I was asked to lead. After the president of the organization I was working for described the current state, I wondered two things. First, the business results were so dire and seemingly impossible to recover from, so why not throw in the towel and redirect precious resources elsewhere where there is more upside potential? Second, why on earth do you think I am the one who can take this on with no experience in doing this kind of work?

I decided not to ask the first question, but I did ask the second. And the answer made me forget about my first question. It was this experience that taught me about the importance of organizational purpose, empathic leadership, and sponsorship. I also learned that change is possible when you meet people where they are, and inspire them to join you on the journey. But, not everyone will be ready and willing to go where you are headed.

Empathy, Organizational Purpose, and Sponsorship

Transformational change represents a significant shift in business strategy, operations, or culture that requires radical changes to the organization's current state. It is typically motivated by internal or external forces that if not addressed, will potentially pose an existential threat to an organization's viability.

Talking about transformational change this way will likely scare the living daylights out of your workforce, causing them to lose focus in their day jobs and run towards the nearest exit. Transformational change leaders recognize that change is much more than a process. It is an experience that generates a wide range of emotions, which is why the most successful leaders approach transformational change with empathy and anchor their change in organizational purpose.

I have always silently cringed when hearing the term "soft" skills particularly when those soft skills are not only hard to develop, demonstrate, and master, but they can make or break a leader. This is particularly true when the leader is faced with leading an organization through major change. Approaching large-scale change with rational reasoning, without explicitly recognizing and tending to the emotional aspects, will immediately reduce the potential for success right out of the gate. Empathic leaders strive to understand the needs of their workforce who bring their histories, perspectives, and cultures to the workplace.

This reality is why diversity and inclusion must be a core component of your transformational change strategy, so that the collective strengths of your organization can be leveraged. Research from McKinsey and Company shows that 70% of organizational transformations fail, and the primary reasons are due to employee resistance and lack of management support.[18] When leaders approach change from an empathic perspective, they are less likely to face resistance and more likely to generate trust and inspiration.

Establishing a strong sense of organizational purpose is foundational to transformational change because it conveys the "why," but this is easier said than done. It requires a relentless commitment to overcommunicating with your workforce and customers so they can visualize the changes you are pursuing, the drivers of change, the consequences of not changing, the opportunities the change will create, and the path and timeframe for realizing the change. Equally important is to convey what is not changing, such as your company values.

Successful change efforts share a common denominator, leader sponsorship. Sponsors are in positions with organizational influence and they can help remove barriers, allocate needed resources, and provide needed emotional support. In addition, they lift you up when the going gets tough.

Build Change Resiliency Throughout the Employee Lifecycle

If you are embarking upon transformational change and realize you need to equip your workforce with change management skills and tools, you are already too late. Leading change while trying to build organizational change capacity is like building the plane while you are already in flight. Building a change resilient organization starts with hiring people who are adaptable and can thrive in a VUCA (Volatile, Uncertain, Complex, and Ambiguous) world.

Resilient people demonstrate flexibility vs. rigidity. They are self-aware and possess strong coping mechanisms when faced with stress or ambiguity. They know how and when to seek the help of others and demonstrate perseverance when the going gets tough. Equip your hiring managers with behavioral interview questions to assess for resilience such as "Tell me about a time when you faced a situation when you had to adapt your behavior in response to changing circumstances." or "When you have faced a stressful situation, how did you respond, what did you do?"

Hiring people who are agile and can adapt to change is a great start, but to be one of the 30% of organizations that succeed at transformational change, you also need to incorporate change management into your people and organizational development programs. Typically change management experts reside in Human Resources and do not get me wrong, they should. But how much more effective will your change effort be if your employees, regardless of role or level, have the knowledge and skills to meaningfully contribute to the transformational change agenda?

I was working in an organization that was merging with another organization. Emotions were high because it did not feel like a merger, but rather a hostile takeover, and it was clear which organization was going to emerge with greater leadership representation and whose business processes would dominate. The Human Resources professionals arrived to provide organizational design expertise wearing their respective team jerseys.

Empathy was absent. We had lost our sense of purpose. Even if we took off our jerseys and created new ones that showed we were united, we needed our business leaders to arrive at the same conclusions. We convinced our respective leaders to participate in an organizational design certification program with us. They agreed and what happened next was transformational in and of itself. Our leaders were now certified in organizational design, inspired by what they learned, and ready to lead. Moral of the story: help your leaders become transformational change practitioners and leaders.

When transformational change needs to occur and there is no sign of a fire anywhere to motivate change, what do you do? In addition to what has already been shared in terms of creating an understanding of the case for change and what is at risk, incentive strategies must be designed to motivate, recognize, and reward change agents (at every level, not just at the top). Create an inclusive environment where everyone can contribute to the purpose and shape the future of the organization, and be recognized for their role.

"Leadership is a Behavior, not a Position"

I cannot exactly recall when or where I first saw this statement, but it has surfaced in one form or another a myriad of times in leadership literature. What I do know is that it has stuck with me and influenced how I have approached leadership development philosophically and programmatically. If every employee is empowered to think, act, and be treated as a leader during times of change, they will. Leadership can be demonstrated by anyone at any level. Transformational change takes a village. Acquire and build a resilient village because the only thing you can count on is change. And it is the collective power of people that makes change possible.

Three Things to Know or Do About Transformational Change

1. Begin and end with leadership empathy.
2. Build organizational change capabilities before they are needed, or it is too late.
3. Embed change resiliency throughout the employee lifecycle.

Mindset in Organizational Transformation

By Jennifer E. McEwen, Ph.D.

Transforming organizations is not easy. Robin Speculand[19] reports the failure rate over the last 15 years as 60–90%. Successful organizational transformation requires a mindset that *all* people in the system are key to the transformation. Singular focus on any one group (e.g., employees or customers) or disjointed efforts between those groups suboptimizes outcomes.

I consult on organizational transformations, often specializing in those that address customer relationship challenges. Sometimes, my expertise is sought only after a transformation does not go well or too much time passes without results. I have identified three principles that take transformations wider, farther, and deeper in their impact. I will share these along with a success story that affirms the value of the principles.

Principle 1 – Go Wider: Align All People in the System

A system of relationships can be described as a people value chain. Whether the objective is to improve employee experience (EX) or customer experience (CX), people experience (PX) is the foundation. Michael Porter's value chain theory[20] highlights the importance of people in the value chain. Today, organizations are realizing the benefit of bringing people into primary focus for transformation success.

Principle 2 – Go Farther: Engage People Beyond the Role They Play

Relationships are at the heart of business. Starting at the top, executives seek to align people in a direction for a desired outcome. Beliefs, ideas, and vision translate to results through people, for people (e.g., through employees for customers). No matter their role, people have common needs and desires at their core. Humans sometimes forget this. When interactions are restricted to the roles people play (e.g., manager, employee, customer) rather than the breadth of what they can contribute, relationships are jeopardized, and people cannot contribute fully. And assumptions made about people, based on a role they play, diminish the potential to strengthen and positively transform a relationship.

Principle 3 – Go Deeper: Embrace Openness and Curiosity to Create New Possibilities

To transform any relationship, it helps to consider how people interact and their reality. Process work by Arnold Mindell[21] defines three distinct levels of reality: Consensus Reality, Dreamland, and Essence. Together, these comprise our experience and offer invaluable insight for change. All levels are equally important. They help explain the potential for biases and conflict which inhibit openness. Organizations tend to focus more on the first two levels, and less on the third.

First, *Consensus Reality* is observable, shareable, and measurable. Consensus makes agreement easier. In the second level, *Dreamland*, people share what is on their mind such as hopes, ideas, and plans. The third level, *Essence*, contains our deeper tendencies that are emotionally felt. *Essence* is intangible and not easily expressed in words. It requires noticing sensations. It is like the atmosphere of a group or relationship. Access to this level is crucial for self-awareness and other-awareness. Awareness requires a mindset of openness and curiosity, which are vital to creating new possibilities for the relationship.

Case Study: A Multi-Billion-Dollar Company With Dissatisfied Customers

The organization's customer shares they lack trust in the company's ability to address their needs. In response, the organization undertakes a large-scale transformation to create greater customer centricity. At the same time, tensions exist between organizational units evidenced by their internal rivalry for business. Company structures hinder collaboration and innovation. People in the organization exhibit derailing behaviors, validating the customer feedback. Despite all this, the CEO insists the transformation focus purely on the *external* customer. The obvious disconnect is not readily apparent to the CEO. His focus is up and out. He has lost touch with what is happening inside the organization.

With customer centricity as the imperative, one C-Suite member of the organization holds a key meeting where the agenda is to brainstorm ways to improve the customer relationship. During the dialogue, one senior executive says, "*Our customers are stupid and don't know what they want!*" The sudden, ghastly look on the meeting sponsor's face clearly indicates she is disturbed by what she just heard. "*What did you just say?!*" she asks. She allows him a split-second to respond, which he cannot fast enough. Then she adds, "*From this point forward, I ask that you not even think that . . . let alone say it!*" Her words pierce like a dart on a bullseye.

This pivotal moment shines a light. It becomes obvious they must approach things differently. The way they feel toward their customer affects their ability to see them as having needs and desires, just as they do. They are not connecting with the customer at the "essence" level, hampering the relationship and its potential to grow. This likely contributes to the customer's perception their needs are not being met. The organization decides not only to change the conversation but also to examine the stories they tell themselves about their customers.

The CEO employs transformation experts. They gather compelling data and stories that confirm the entire system of people must be aligned for the transformation to succeed. In a tipping point moment, the CEO finally acknowledges that "customer" must be redefined. This will now comprise any person in the organizational system who receives value from another, including employees. The experts begin to assess relationship systems in the value chain.

Their transformation becomes holistic. It adds focus on cultural changes needed to restore organizational health and improve relationships across the system. Below are examples of tactical actions they took as they worked through the broader organizational transformation using the framework described in the next section.

- They reset expectations around their core values. These had been touted for decades, but not demonstrated in people's behavior. The goal: Live these core values every day, in every way.
- They enhanced their traditional diversity and inclusion programs to emphasize the value of leadership in creating inclusion throughout the work process.
- They articulated desired behaviors (e.g., listening, openness and curiosity, inquiry, acknowledgment, and reflection) and provided coaching to reinforce using those behaviors for productive interactions.
- They established a governance structure to enable intentional collaboration and drive greater innovation. This forum was used to share success stories from relating differently.
- They aligned engagement measures for both employees and external customers. This allowed the organization to see patterns between the two and adjust where needed.

Eventually, they crack the code for customer centricity and transform their organization. They see vast improvements in relationships within two years. Three years later, their stock value more than quadruples organically. The organization continues to maintain a high level of performance and success today. They did this using a four-step organizational transformation framework.

The Organizational Transformation Framework

The organizational transformation framework is straightforward. It is based on Roger Connors' and Tom Smith's[22] work, aimed at creating experiences that foster beliefs, drive actions, and produce desired results. I expanded this to incorporate leadership best practices and principles from Organization and Relationship Systems Coaching (ORSC™)[23] to create lasting change through people. This framework has been proven effective in many organizational transformations, including one documented in a *Harvard Business School*[4] case study that outlines a similar "people first" approach.

1. *Beliefs* . . . Start with purpose, clarify what is believed, and identify what is valued and prioritized.
2. *Experiences* . . . Understand current experiences, improve experiences where desired, and repeat positive experiences.
3. *Actions* . . . Practice desired behaviors of leadership in all interactions and share success stories.
4. *Results* . . . Celebrate strengthened relationships that support desired outcomes and be open to new possibilities through every engagement.

In summary, for organizational transformation to be successful and lasting, it requires all people in the system to be aligned. People have different experiences, beliefs, preferences towards action, and ideas for results that merit engaging them beyond their designated role. Finally, adopting a mindset of openness and curiosity creates new possibilities for transformation success.

Three Things to Know or Do About Transformational Change

1. Go wider: All people in the system must be engaged for success in any one area.
2. Go farther: Interacting beyond the roles people play allows people greater contribution.
3. Go deeper: Openness and curiosity heighten understanding and create new possibilities.

Transformation in Action

By Dermot O'Brien

Catalyst for Change

We have heard it before, never let a crisis go to waste; well that was the wagon we hitched our latest transformation to following a proxy fight with a hedge fund. They underestimated our CEO, Carlos Rodriguez, and ADP's investor support and lost the proxy battle by a large margin. That process did, however, involve ADP making some big financial commitments over the following three fiscal years (June to July 2018–2021) and was the catalyst behind the creation of a new role, Chief Transformation Officer, that I held for over three years.

While there had always been a great deal of pride at ADP in our ability to transform to meet the needs of the market over many decades, we wanted the process to be focused and sustainable; we believed that with a dedicated Transformation Office, we could pursue a more deliberate process of reinvention to manage the company's future in the best long-term interests of our various stakeholders.

Purpose by Design

I get asked all the time how did we do it, how did we know if it would work? There was no playbook initially, just promises that needed to be met. Carlos tapped me from the executive team given his experience with how HR had transformed itself and its impact on ADP's Talent and Business Performance over the prior six years. He observed "how" we made changes, not just "what" changes we made. We had high expectations, but worked as a global team for the first time and treated people with respect, even when and especially when people moved on from the organization.

Before we defined what we were going to transform, I sent out a few brief personal videos to all 60,000 associates that simply focused on how we were going to approach the changes, by living our well-established values, particularly, Each Person Counts. In hindsight, these early messages on our culture and values proved key to garnering the support of our people to embrace the changes that were to follow. The communications also helped associates hold leadership accountable to the "how" standard we had reinforced through these early video messages.

I also shared a quote that was framed on Herb Allison's desk (my first CEO at TIAA), "The more you want things to stay the same, the more things need to Change."

Define Success: What Is the Game and How Do You Keep Score?

If you do not have a vision and a plan, be careful, as you may end up there! It feels like every large company has a transformation underway and yet we hear about the consultant studies that highlight failed transformation efforts. If you want 60,000 people to work together you need to Keep It Simple and Define Success, then measure and share, openly and regularly, how things are going. Transparency is key. We rise and fall together.

I always say, people are smart, but organizations are dumb! It is a reminder to keep things simple. I started my early messaging by saying the Transformation Office was going to focus on Two Key Areas; A group of nine goals under a rallying brand named Win-as-One, and a living set of Initiatives that would support the achievement of the nine Win-as-One goals. That was it, two areas of focus: nine corporate goals and an evolving list of initiatives in support of those goals. This is "what" we focused on as a company for an initial period of three years.

If You Want to Change Outcomes, Change the Routines

Once you have set the Vision/Purpose you should set an operating cadence that gets people involved, captures needed information, helps with decision making, and shares successes and failures frequently. Designing accountability into your plan is essential.

From the start, we set up a biweekly two-hour cadence with the executive committee, including the CEO. These meetings quickly became must-attend sessions and many even attended while on vacation to make sure they did not miss out on the latest decisions. We reported quarterly to the entire company how we were doing on the nine goals and this report-out was through an online Win-as-One blog from our CEO, Carlos. He would personally respond to every comment and question that came his way, demonstrating his personal ownership and commitment to ADP's Transformation Agenda.

Carlos had developed a simple lens a number of years prior that he shared with our global associates so they would understand how he looked at the business. It was Simplify, Innovate, and Grow. Our nine goals, three each, were put under this familiar lens to aid in common understanding and connection of our efforts.

Very early on, we wanted to connect these goals to our incentive plans and quickly mobilized an approach that tied bonus compensation for the executive committee to our nine goals. We also tied all bonus eligible associates to the Client Net Promoter Score (NPS) goal we had set for the company (Division results did not count here, only what we all achieved together as a company). This NPS result affected 25% of their bonus.

For the remaining half of the organization that was not bonus eligible, we put in place a special annual payout of 0–5% of salary if two conditions were met; 1. We exceeded the profit goals we had set (this helped us fund the payout) and 2. We met or exceeded our company-wide Client NPS goal. This way, if our clients were happy and we had "extra" money, we could all Win-as-One.

Nothing made me happier than to include everyone in our thinking and we ended up having a 4% payout in fiscal 2019 and a maximum 5% payout in fiscal 2021. COVID-19 created financial headwinds in fiscal 2020 that resulted in no payout. Our associates understood and we literally heard no complaints given all the other amazing things ADP set in motion during the pandemic to support our associates and their families.

The biweekly meetings with the executive team had a laser-like focus on results from our initiatives and the decisions we needed to make to clear any blockage in the system. Our initiatives covered about 50 projects covering Cost, Growth, and Competition under categories such as Organizational Agility (spans and layers, early retirement plan), Revenue Growth, Competitive Positioning (pricing, market share, new products), Digital Transformation, and Procurement Optimization.

Set a High Bar!

It takes courage to achieve what has never been achieved before and that means taking a risk by setting a high bar for results. What is transformation anyway? In our case, we defined it as a Step Change in Performance.

To give you an idea of how high we set the bar, the three Win-as-One goals under the "Grow" heading were: 1. Achieve the highest level ever in client retention, 2. Improve overall ADP Client NPS by 100%, and 3. Deliver Adjusted EBIT (Earnings Before Interest and Taxes) growth that was two and half times the growth of the prior several years. All nine Win-as-One goals were BIG and that has made all the difference in getting people's attention.

Our Transformation goals and related Transformation Initiatives were not activities that were off to the side, they were the business and the focus of the Board, CEO, Executive Committee, and all leaders and associates around the globe. We designed our approach holistically from the start, adapted quickly along the way, had a senior team that worked well together, and were led by a CEO who was 100% supportive. Of course, that just does not happen by itself. You need to nurture it through confidence and healthy relationship building.

An amazing thing happens as people and ideas get mobilized and then implemented, positive results start to show, and people gain more and more confidence in both their abilities and the company's ability to make big and fast changes. A certain confidence, or dare I say swagger, can be observed. The quadrupling of ADP's stock price while I was with ADP seemed to be a clear reflection of the market's recognition of the value of our team's great efforts over those nine years.

Take care of your clients with great products and services while taking care of your employees, and the financials will take care of themselves.

Three Things to Know or Do About Transformational Change

1. *Define Success*: Set a high-performance bar of measurable outcomes supported by detailed business cases, that include change management plans.
2. *Include Everyone*: Make everyone feel like they are involved and helping. Importantly, reward them.
3. *Be Transparent*: Share results openly and regularly.

Characteristics of a Resilient Organization

By Cheryl Perkins

In 2020, the pandemic challenged many organizations to redesign the way they operate, rethink the goods and services they provide, and refresh their brand's messaging as COVID-19 packed a decade's worth of disruption into just a few short months. While the organizations that were nimble enough to make these changes quickly have set themselves up for long-term success, the organizations that were unable to swiftly adapt to our new reality struggled. As I observed leaders across every industry navigate through the uncertainty of COVID-19, it became clear that the organizations that were successful all had one thing in common: they had proactive systems and processes in place that increased their resilience.

In this essay, we will unpack what it means to be a resilient organization, explore the key characteristics resilient organizations have in common, and provide tips to help you create long-term stability for your company.

What Is a Resilient Organization?

A resilient organization is one that prepares for, responds to, and adapts to incremental changes and sudden disruptions in order to not only survive but prosper. These organizations go beyond the typical risk management protocol and focus on a more holistic view of their organization's overall health and success. This helps them do more than just survive in the face of adversity; it helps them thrive and set themselves up for long-term growth.

By examining the organizations that did more than simply sustain themselves throughout the pandemic, we can learn a great deal about how to proactively prepare our organizations for the unexpected and inevitable change in the future.

What Are Some Key Benefits of Being a Resilient Organization?

Besides being better equipped to handle unexpected challenges, some of the key benefits of being a resilient organization include:

- *Higher job satisfaction:* Studies show that employees who work for resilient organizations report lower levels of stress and higher levels of job satisfaction. Resilient organizations can offer employees more stability and resources, which can increase employee retention rates.
- *Increased capacity:* Resilient organizations often invest in processes, systems, and training for their team that increase their capacity to produce

quality products and services. Investing in your team can also lead to new, innovative breakthroughs for your organization.

- *More effective management:* Being a resilient organization requires leaders within the company to share common goals and strategies. This can help unify management and provide your team with a clear set of expectations and goals.
- *More engaged culture:* Resilient organizations also understand the importance of encouraging teamwork, promoting creative problem-solving, and rewarding employees who do well. In return, employees are often more engaged with the work they do.

Important Organizational Elements to Focus on

The three most important elements we see resilient organizations focus on are people, products, and processes. An organization cannot be truly resilient or sustainable if they lack the resources and dedication that are necessary to invest in each of these areas. Let us take a closer look at how these elements build the foundation of an organization's ecosystem:

- *Employee behavior:* Your people are the driving force behind your products, services, customer relationships, and strategic and innovative developments. To successfully navigate unexpected changes as an organization, you need to ensure your team has the physical, mental, and emotional capacity to adapt. Consider how you can support your team to create more flexibility and encourage their problem-solving skills.
- *Product excellence:* Ensuring product excellence is critical during uncertain times because it can determine whether your consumers will continue purchasing from you. Listen to your consumers' needs, innovate with them in mind, and continually evaluate feedback to ensure your organization is adapting to incremental changes.
- *Process reliability:* Processes must be adaptable, yet reliable, in order to provide consistent products and services to consumers. Listen to your team's feedback to identify areas of improvement. Then develop a plan to implement these changes. By continuously investing in process development, your organization may be better positioned to navigate unexpected changes when they occur.

What Are Some of the Key Characteristics of a Resilient Organization?

Here are some of the key characteristics I have observed in resilient organizations across all industries:

Strong Leadership

In resilient organizations, leadership is not just a title, it is a responsibility. Throughout the pandemic, I have observed many leaders navigate quick decisions that allowed them to lead their teams through uncertainty, even when they did not have all the information they would have liked. These leaders understand that you cannot be paralyzed by indecision when swift action is required. We can never be 100% informed about any decision we make, but as leaders, we must be willing to step outside of our comfort zones to move forward. This type of leadership allows us to grow, adapt, and innovate.

Unified Human Resources

An effective human resources team is one that collaborates with other thought leaders at every level of the organization. Companies that embrace this holistic approach to human resources develop stronger communication across their team, ensure that leaders share common objectives, and promote a culture that embodies the same values and goals. This alignment can help increase workplace morale and encourage teamwork, which are essential when challenges arise.

Risk Mitigation

In times of crisis, customers, consumers, and businesses carefully evaluate purchases, but history shows us that when the economy stumbles badly, innovative companies use this as an opportunity to create and deliver breakthrough innovation. Analyzing data about your organization, workforce, products, and processes can help you identify pain points and challenges. This can help you determine which risks are worth taking without halting all the new programs, processes, or innovative developments that may lead to future growth.

Adaptive Thinking

For many businesses, the pandemic lowered customer spending and increased supply chain costs. To weather this storm, resilient organizations focused on connecting with their consumers at an emotional level to identify their needs. Then, they adapted their services, products, and messaging to meet these needs. Organizations that saw the most success with these tactics already encouraged this type of adaptive thinking in their employees before the pandemic by rewarding employees who developed creative solutions. Cultivating this skill set in your workforce can help you adjust quickly to changes in the market.

A Culture of Well-Being

When change inevitably occurs, pay attention to how it impacts your team. Resilient organizations proactively fight against change fatigue, which can present itself through a wide range of mental and physical issues, including anxiety and burnout. Consider what programs, incentives, or positive reinforcement you can provide to improve your team's overall well-being. This may also involve analyzing what practices are detrimental to your culture. Small details like frequently contacting employees outside of their normal office hours can have a significant negative impact on your organization's workforce and overall happiness.

An Investment in Professional Development

Successful leaders develop their talent through selective skill-based hiring and continuous training. Investing in your employees by providing them with opportunities to hone their skills and learn new things can increase the quality of your products and services. It can also promote creative thinking, problem-solving, and adaptability. Equip your team with a wide range of skill sets to make your organization more resilient to change.

Strong Partnerships and Alliances

Many leaders are embracing open innovation by forming strategic partnerships and alliances with inventors, entrepreneurs, suppliers, vendors, academic institutions, and other organizations, including competitors. Time and time again we see the benefits of soliciting ideas from outside organizations. Collaborating with others can reduce costs, lower risk levels, provide more resources, and increase your speed to market. If exploring external partnerships interests you, start by assessing the internal competencies required to deliver on your business objectives. This can help you determine where your company's internal strengths and weaknesses are. Then consider which partners may provide you with the resources you lack to fill in these gaps.

Crisis prompts us to think differently, and strong leadership becomes critical during uncertain times. As business leaders, we may not know what the next event that challenges our organization will be, but we can take steps to better prepare ourselves.

Three Things to Know or Do About Transformational Change

1. *Assess your core capabilities:* Successful organizations are prepared for change because they understand what their strengths and resources are. This knowledge can help you be proactive and adaptable when faced with a crisis.
2. *Use your resources responsibly:* Resilient organizations understand the importance of funding innovative endeavors and strategic business plans. Instead of restricting your resources during a crisis, consider what the best use of your resources is to promote long-term growth and stability.
3. *Encourage teamwork:* Highly resilient organizations encourage teamwork across all levels of their company. Consider who the key players are on your team and how you can create a work environment that encourages them to collaborate together.

A Compelling Vision Is Not Enough

By Patrick R. Powaser, Ph.D.

Having a compelling vision for transforming an organization is necessary for success, but vision alone will not make the change happen. As the environment changed around a historically successful company, the organization and its employees needed to change as well. Skill-building in conflict management and decision-making helped drive changes in the company's culture. A new organization structure and top management opened doors for employees to develop themselves and more fully contribute to the organization's success.

Time for Change

LatPetro,[25] the South American division of a global energy company, had been the crown jewel in the parent company's diverse portfolio for decades. Its production, revenues, and relationship with the local government were models for other divisions and companies.

Oscar, the general manager, relied on his many years of experience to direct the operations of the company from his office perched on the top floor of the headquarters building. All major decisions, and many minor decisions, were made on that floor. Directives were issued to managers and, sometimes, even individual employees. Employees had clarity on what was expected of them and performed well on the work they were assigned.

That model worked well for years. And then the environment around Lat-Petro started to shift. The host governments wanted greater partnership and sharing. The technology required to efficiently produce hydrocarbons demanded better-qualified employees. The old organizational structure no longer fit the pressures on the company. Employees were being recruited by other energy companies and were walking away to take new jobs.

The parent company realized that change at LatPetro needed to start from the top. Oscar had produced outstanding results for many years. He was now surrounded by an environment that looked very different than when he started with the company. He scheduled his retirement and prepared to step aside from the organization he had largely built.

Oscar's successor, Daniel, was both a technical whiz and a firm believer that strong leaders needed to surround themselves with strong teams. During his career, Daniel had worked around the globe and had proudly built teams that he described as "a lot smarter than I was." And he encouraged employees to find their own paths to success.

Shortly after Daniel took the reins, he and I talked about changes he thought were necessary in his organization. He said he had a vision for the direction he wanted to take the company and for the aggressive results of which he thought the company was capable. He shared that he needed help figuring out how to get where he envisioned taking the company, including unleashing the collective experience and knowledge of the employees. But, a compelling vision alone was not enough. We collaborated to explore what likely needed to change, including the organization's structure, culture, decision-making, and accountability.

Culture Drives Results

Culture is a combination of acceptable and expected behaviors, along with systems and processes that are part of the everyday work environment. There is a saying that if you want to change business results, you must change the organization's culture.

We asked Daniel to share the ideal organization culture to support his vision for the company. To do so, we used a tool called the Organizational Culture Inventory (OCI).[26] OCI measures 12 dimensions of workplace behaviors and groups those dimensions into three clusters:

- **Constructive:** achieving goals by focusing on people development and maximizing individual and group contributions.
- **Aggressive/Defensive:** focusing on one's own needs and achievements versus the success of the team.
- **Passive/Defensive:** giving in to the demands of management and the organization at the expense of individual contribution and growth.

Daniel completed the OCI with his vision in mind. Consistent with his goal of maximizing employee contribution and supporting individual growth and development, the **Constructive** cluster was very pronounced while the two **Defensive** clusters were minimized.

We then asked each employee to complete the OCI describing the culture as they currently experienced it. As we expected, the composite results were largely the opposite of Daniel's vision. The **Defensive** clusters were maximized, and the **Constructive** cluster was minimized. We had a lot of work to do and a lot of history to overcome.

Daniel organized a town hall meeting to gather as many employees as possible in one room. He wanted them to hear his vision and his expectations. After he shared his thoughts, we broke out into smaller groups, asked each group to share what they heard, and recorded their ideas on how to get there. We then asked them to draw pictures of what success would look like and when it would occur. Many drew mountains with joyful employees jumping up and down at the peak. The feelings of excitement and the anticipation of working a different way were thick in the room. The teams were aggressive on their timelines and eager to make changes that benefited them, the company, and the community.

Conflict Can Be Good

Historically, there had been little substantial conflict within the organization because of the top-down, directive management style. With the new vision and new culture, we explored with the employees and the senior team what conflict might look like, how it might impact the organization, and strategies for finding the positives in different points of view. We worked with individual teams to identify their primary means of dealing with conflict through the TKI tool.[27] TKI measures five different conflict modes/styles and helps individuals identify their primary way of dealing with conflict. The five modes are:

- Avoiding
- Accommodating
- Compromising
- Competing
- Collaborating

While the word "conflict" often generates a negative connotation, we explored the positives and benefits of having different perspectives on the same issue. We also explored when each of these modes would be appropriate and how to recognize a disconnect between the situation and one's preferred mode.

We led multiple discovery sessions during which the team members learned how to identify conflict, select the most effective style to use for a given conflict, and then practiced effectively handling conflict in different situations. Employees described using their newfound insights and skills, both at work and outside of work, to find the positives in everyday conflict.

Decisions and Accountability

Joyous cries of "We get to make decisions!" punctuated our next set of team meetings. I vividly remember thinking how profound that statement was. Recall that in the past, decision-making was centralized, and most employees did not have the opportunity to participate. Capitalizing on the teams' energy, we explored questions like "What kinds of decisions are you most looking forward to making?" "Which decisions might be difficult to make?" and "What are your options for making decisions?" The latter question was immediately answered with "We'll make all decisions by consensus!" With further conversation, the teams ended up committing to make as many decisions as possible by consensus, but also realized some decisions simply needed to be made and then communicated broadly.

Another wrinkle in having decision-making authority is taking responsibility for what has been decided. This was a new way of working for the employees. We worked through the process of decision-making, communication, celebrating successes, and owning failures.

Restructure

As with many energy companies, functions worked in distinct silos. Engineering, Finance, Production, Marketing, IT, HR, and others worked issues up and down their columns with little knowledge or concern of what impact they might have on other parts of the company. Based on his prior experience, Daniel and his team took down the silos and rebuilt the organization with cross-functional teams. Alignment and communication were enhanced, and production increased.

Business Results

Eighteen months into the transformation, business results were stronger than ever. Production and revenues were up, safety incidents were down, host governments were pleased, and employees had renewed reasons to stay with the company. Daniel expressed his appreciation for the assistance he received, and the parent company was able to use LatPetro's experience to drive change in other divisions of the corporation.

Three Things to Know or Do About Transformational Change

1. Maintain a keen focus on the vision.
2. Engage employees at all levels of the organization.
3. Treat the journey as an experiment and adjust as necessary at every step along the way.

Designing Our Future: Transformational Change Requires Strategic Foresight

By Linda Rogers and Tessa Finlev

Our future does not have a singular owner or a predetermined blueprint. Each of us has the power to influence and a shared responsibility to intentionally design our future.

Transformational change requires comfort in designing in the unknown. It is about creating confidence, based on information we collect, questions we contemplate, and assumptions we must make, to articulate a clear vision for an intentional future.

Enabling transformational change is about knowing that there is no final destination; you are on a continuous journey. One that is very rarely a straight path. There are tangents, diversions, and collisions. It requires adapting, accepting, and learning from the unpredictable. All of which lead us to an understanding of what our future might be.

COVID-19 forced us all through immediate and continuous transformative change. We have had to evaluate life and work through a redefined lens, ask new questions, and contemplate differently what our future might be.

While accelerated by COVID-19, our deep familiarity with transformational change is not solely attributed to the coronavirus pandemic. There has been much ongoing change. Technological advances and disruptions, climate change and volatility, and the changing nature of where, what, when, and how we work have been longtime forcing mechanisms of change.

Over the past 18 months, transformation was forced to the forefront and needed to be confronted. When under the pressures of extreme uncertainty and change, companies had to rapidly learn, unlearn, and relearn how to support their people, adapt their role as a corporate citizen, and drive their businesses.

In this present moment when the world feels deeply messy, uncertain, and noisy, lies the opportunity to architect the future. While none of us have a crystal ball or know exactly where all this will end up, we do know that the basic principles we have been relying on for the last century to organize and get things done are not the most effective anymore.

It is ever present that companies need to actively design desirable, cool, delightful futures, or risk being left behind. To effectively break through and create continuous value, companies must ideate toward an intentional future. And, this is the magic of an internal foresight capacity, the ability to effectively imagine possible futures.

Strategic Foresight

Strategic foresight is a fundamental skill set for all businesses. This work stretches beyond predictions and creates the muscle for organizations to put structure around how to design their desired future and understand what possible future will come from the new products or services they create. By systematically researching possible futures and designing critical conversations for how those futures might impact strategy, organizational identity, culture, and talent, companies can find clarity and develop a sense of control over their futures. This design work enables future planning and clarity even in light of powerful external forces of change.

The process is a dance between understanding where the external world is going, internal capabilities, and strategic ambition. It is an internally driven form of continuous transformational change that unlocks the ability to become agile experimenters. During transformational times, strategic foresight helps us gain clarity about what is possible, and it enhances our own abilities to transform.

Developing foresight establishes a process to contemplate plausible possibilities, develop hope for the future, and power our ability to act and transform. It is a path that challenges the status quo and asks us to adopt different ways of thinking, discover new possibilities, and unlock new ways of doing.

At Dolby, our People and Places team has undergone a major transformation to grow our own comfort in being agile experimenters. In our role as the organization's talent guide, we know our people and our capabilities are the magic that create the future of sight and sound experiences for the world. Our people are the inventors of our business' future. As we act as stewards of our culture and organizational designs, we seek to enable our networks to see around corners and be at the ready to adapt our workflows and areas of expertise to new and emergent possibilities.

Futures Council

As part of our enablement, we launched an internal Futures Council. The role of this group is to dedicate mindshare to research possible futures and anticipate emergent futures. They connect the dots and find patterns that may not otherwise be obvious and invoke the art of storytelling to create action.

Our Futures Council scans the external environment and connects elements back to Dolby. This process enables us to act with intention and explore what is possible, from weird to awesome, so that we can design a future that aligns with our capabilities, strategic ambition, and what the world wants.

Dolby's Futures Council is a companywide network with domain experts who represent all our businesses, functions, and market segments. It comprises individuals with broad, multi-disciplinary, and horizontal network connections, and participants are asked to research, understand, and weigh in on future trends most relevant to our business focus areas. The group brings the big complex questions to the forefront and assesses developing future trends through the Dolby lens. Is it impactful to Dolby? Is there a potential market there? What might the time to market be? How disruptive might it be?

Understanding possible futures is not a straightforward task. It requires that we address our own biases, assumptions, and existing mental models. It requires that we move away from reactive thinking toward being able to understand things that we have never imagined. It demands a humble willingness to learn and, at times, to let go of expertise.

In today's world of hyper-competition and constant flux, we need to be thinking ten steps or ten years ahead. We are past the times of assuming that anything will remain stable. The ability for the world to change in an instant has become and will remain ever present.

Being ready to receive new information that breaks understood patterns, and then make sense of it, is a valuable skill we need to invest in. Strategic foresight is complex and deeply challenging thinking. When we successfully build and support a large community of forward-thinking people within a company, we gain access to a collective mind that will enable transformational change, whether internally or externally driven.

Three Things to Know or Do About Transformational Change

1. **Look long, see around corners, and be a dot connector.** It is critical to look around corners and identify patterns across all elements of the world you belong to. This capability enables you to develop a point of view on transformational change and emergent futures.

2. **Be a people activator.** Enable others to see and be a part of understanding and co-creating what the future can be. Transformational change happens faster and smoother when we mobilize as many people as possible.

3. **Be a change agent. Always.** All change requires the courage to act. Moving towards change requires conviction to make decisions, even in the face of uncertainty. Creating a vision of where we are going that is inspirational, provides clarity, and has been developed in a collaborative way, enables our collective ability to act for change.

Transforming Performance Management: And Making It Stick

By Deb Seidman

Many change efforts fail to sustain new behaviors. Unlike other change initiatives, a creative Human Resources team embedded value-added performance management processes, tools, and mindsets in the business that have stood the test of time. Three key levers made the difference: 1) having a compelling "why" 2) partnering with business leaders to create business-driven people practices and tools that will enable strategy execution, and 3) making the process and tools user friendly to facilitate adoption.

The Opportunity

The executive team of a leading, global commercial bank had made the strategic decision to transform the bank into a bulge-bracket investment bank. Doing so meant selling off parts of the commercial banking operations and building up the corporate banking and capital markets sides of the business. A strategy consulting firm was brought in to undertake cost-restructuring efforts and advise on the management practices needed to support the new business strategy.

The strategy firm recommended adopting a set of performance management practices and tools used by professional services firms. These included:

- Role/Skill grids: Documents that specified the key skills needed for roles at each level in the hierarchy and described what constituted unsatisfactory, satisfactory, and outstanding performance of those skills
- Team reviews: Mechanisms by which a manager could collect performance feedback from those who worked on deals with his/her direct reports
- Evaluation Committees: Performance calibration discussions to rate and rank people's performance for application to pay-for-performance incentive compensation decisions

The firm's executives established the expectation that every area of the firm, covering approximately 25,000 employees, would deploy these performance management tools.

Prior to this change, performance management consisted of completing an end-of-year evaluation document which was seen as an administrative exercise unrelated to what mattered for the business and largely divorced from informing compensation decisions. The information documented in the performance evaluation was not considered useful or accurate. A person's compensation level was assumed to be the true indicator of their performance, not the performance review, even though other factors such as market for the role and overall bonus funding had a significant impact on an individual's pay.

We, in HR, were asked to dust off the old annual performance evaluation form and build the tools the business leaders needed, starting with the development of role/skill grids.

The Transformational Change Narrative (the "Why")

Recognizing that this initiative would require shifting behaviors and mindsets, we started by reframing our work from evaluation as the objective, to effectively managing performance as the objective. We knew that performance management tools would support the process, but they were not an end in themselves. Our messaging about the new performance management approach made it clear that we were making a deliberate shift from an administrative, time-consuming, non-value-added process to one that was business driven and critical for achieving business objectives.

Points of Leverage

The sample role/skill grids that the strategy firm shared with us were deeply flawed in that they did little more than describe performance levels as "unsatisfactory," "good," "outstanding," and "ready for promotion." They did not describe the actual behaviors a person should demonstrate at each level.

We decided to create competency models that highlighted the key competencies necessary for the role, and behaviorally anchored scales that distinguished the behaviors of top performers, satisfactory performers, and poor performers.

Our initial plan was to create a core, firm-wide role/skill grid that would then be tailored to each business and function. However, leadership recognized that there was likely to be little buy-in for a generic model and recommended that we take the opposite approach to start with business areas that were interested in being early adopters, demonstrate the value, and scale up from there.

Fortunately, there were business leaders who were anxious to understand what differentiated top performance from average performance, and they partnered with our HR team to develop role/skill grids for various roles in their organizations. Importantly, we engaged the people who would be using the tools in their development.

We conducted working sessions with managers in the Legal function, where they identified the behaviors that they saw highly effective lawyers demonstrating which differentiated their performance from most other lawyers. Using a different approach, we interviewed people in sales, trading, research, and administrative roles in a capital markets business about how they approached their work and identified performance differentiating behaviors in those roles.

Once the use of these role/skill grids was introduced, we heard from managers that behaviors described gave them the language they needed for meaningful performance conversations with their direct reports, whether setting performance expectations or giving constructive feedback.

In addition to those leaders who were early adopters, the senior leadership of the firm set the expectation that all businesses and functions must create similar grids. Taken together (the positive experience of early adopters and the call to action from senior leadership), there was a "pull" from business users for the new tools, rather than a push from HR.

Facilitating Adoption

We recognized that the tools alone would not shift mindsets and behaviors toward implementing a comprehensive approach to performance management that included setting goals/expectations up front, capturing feedback from relevant sources, and having regular performance and development conversations. We actively sought ways to make the process and the use of the tools as user-friendly as possible to facilitate adoption.

Working with our IT department, we facilitated the workflow for capturing performance feedback and creating performance evaluations. Also, we provided online help (in the form of pop-up screens for help in completing forms) for users to reference as they moved through the process.

Shifting Behaviors

Effective feedback is probably the most important performance management outcome, yet giving constructive feedback is often a challenge for reviewers. We knew that skill-building would be critical to success, so we trained people in giving and receiving feedback and we provided examples of effective written feedback for people to reference.

However, a year-end evaluative process meant that feedback was collected toward the end of the performance year. At that point, managers would first learn of issues that could have been addressed earlier. Also, they were put in a position of having to give feedback to their direct report that differed from the messages they had been sending all year.

To create a proactive performance management process, feedback needed to be in real time and people needed to hear it from the source. We encouraged feedback givers to share the feedback they were sending to the manager directly with the person they were reviewing, and not wait to do so at the end of the year. We made the case for ongoing performance feedback and started to see evidence of more frequent performance conversations, focused on continuous improvement, between peers and between managers and their direct reports.

Little by little, mindsets and behaviors shifted. We transformed from conducting a purely administrative end-of-year evaluation process to managing performance throughout the year, including reviewing goals and expectations as situations evolved, having ongoing feedback conversations, and being thoughtful and deliberate about professional development.

Then Things Changed

As with all change initiatives, the environment within which a change is introduced continues to evolve. That was the case for us. The bank merged with another financial institution and human capital practices merged as well. This meant new forms and new systems. However, much of what we put in place continued post-merger such as the collection of performance feedback from those closest to the person performing the work and performance calibration sessions to inform pay-for-performance compensation decisions. The leaders who had embedded these practices brought them to their new organizations.

While role/skill grids were not formally used in the new process, managers held onto them and continued to reference them for expectation setting and performance feedback.

Years later, we learned that managers who had joined new companies brought the performance management mindsets, practices, and tools they had been using to their new organizations. The value was evident to them and now they were driving the change in their new companies.

Three Things to Know or Do About Transformational Change

1. Identify change champions: This included both executive champions and the early adopters who capitalized on the opportunity to build processes and tools that would support the execution of their business goals.
2. Build positive energy: By working with businesses and functions that wanted to embrace new approaches, we were able to co-create processes and tools with those who had a clear and compelling "why" for the effort.
3. Ensure usefulness: We looked for ways to make it easy. We worked with those who would use the tools so that information was in their language and the process fit with how they conduct business.

The Transformation Playbook

By Padma Thiruvengadam

In a rapidly changing world of technological advances, blurring of industry lines and changes in customer needs and consumer priorities have played an important role in company transformation playbooks. While the need for competitive differentiation remains a key factor, other challenges have recently come to the forefront: environmental, social, geo-politics, employees, to name a few.

Companies are seeking to be more agile. They see the need to balance standardization and personalization, for consumers and employees. While most companies have actively planned to transform, these transformations need to shift from being "events" to being embedded into the thread of organizational evolution. Taking an ongoing inventory of the company's position is critical to its agile journey.

Organizational Inventory

I have found that assessments of the following four categories have been critical not only to understanding the current status, but to building an agile approach:

- **External Market Place**: Some key areas to assess, including impact, are competitors, geo-politics, talent, products, technology, etc. This inventory helps a company better understand to what extent various factors positively or adversely impact the company, what it can control, cost and investment impacts, organic versus inorganic growth and partnership strategies, and approaches to manufacturing or service provision.
- **Portfolio**: Understanding a company's current offering, how it stacks up to its competitors, important shifts, as well as other potential industries to enter.
- **Operations** (Key Business Processes): An objective understanding of key business processes is essential. Information flow and decision rights are deeply tied to processes, thus driving culture. Ensuring that processes are not impediments, but enablers, is critical to transformation and building an agile organization.
- **Capability Requirements**: Understanding current capabilities, organizational structure, strengths, and gaps is an important basis to determine the efficacy of the operating model and talent needs.

A strategy built with a deep understanding of the above provides clarity on where a company wants to differentiate itself and what it will take to deliver the differentiation for maximum impact. Companies typically create their strategy, portfolio prioritization, process improvement, and talent needs in a sequential manner. The highest impact I have had in the organizational inventory process is in understanding the current state and determining the future state, by including colleagues from various parts of the organization. This approach allows for the voices of the employees and champions to be heard and incorporated.

Organization assessment of the following segments of one's company is the first step:

- External Factors
- Portfolio Offering
- Processes
- People

An organizational inventory ensures the intimate interconnectedness among these factors is leveraged with a design thinking approach to planning, and system thinking approach to implementation.

An organizational inventory assessment also offers an opportunity to develop an integrated plan, not only at the enterprise level but deeper in the organization. It allows you to test and refresh your organization's purpose – what we aspire to do as our true north – and offers a broad spectrum for articulating a company's identity through the interplay between these five segments of the company's processes:

- Strategic Priorities
- Operating Plan
- Operating Model & Structure
- Talent Plan
- Portfolio Lifecycle & Commercial Strategy

It also helps define what success will look like for various stakeholders and clarifies links to its KPIs, metrics, and reward mechanisms.

When strategic priorities are clearly articulated, breaking them down to annual and quarterly objectives across the value chain is simplified. This step translates to team and individual objectives and enables the clear articulation of how performance will be measured and rewarded. While there are many aspects to transformation, product offering, technology, data and digital, channel and channel conflict management, and many others, we will focus here on people capabilities and bringing the culture to life.

People Capabilities and Culture

Purpose defines what we aspire to do. Values are the DNA of who we want to become. Behaviors are how we always conduct ourselves with all our stakeholders. As a part of transformation and being an agile organization, we should periodically pressure test these three dimensions to ensure they enable a company's relevance and long-term success.

The operating model should inform the organization's structure, process enhancements, and management routines. Once you understand your immediate and long-term objectives and your key processes that enable your business to operate, evaluate your current organization structure to:

- Determine key capabilities that already exist and new capabilities that are needed, including the impact of technology
- Confirm whether you have the right roles
- Identify the most critical roles with greatest impact and determine if they are at the right level in your organization structure
- Ensure it supports your key processes

This analysis will help determine if your structure will support the delivery of your operational processes and core critical capabilities (please refer to Figure 5.1). It will also help identify gaps that you can proactively address to manage various external and internal factors, including where you need to make adjustments.

In a world where products can be replicated, talent has become a key differentiator. In some instances, a competitive advantage. Having a well-articulated talent ecosystem is fundamental. A talent ecosystem allows for adjustment to skill requirements over time. For simplicity, I usually segment skills into three categories:

1. Essential skills that are embedded in every role in the company. They are critical to bringing to life how work gets done, are the common thread across the company culture, and allow for local contextualization.
2. Functional skills which focus on each area of expertise and depth of expertise needed in that part of the function are often key elements of transformation.
3. Management skills required for leading initiatives, projects or assignments, and delivering on the culture.

Once these skills are shaped, it is important to identify "Distinguishing Skills." Distinguishing Skills help differentiate a company from others. They often deliver a high percentage of value for the company.

Skill requirements and their evolution form the foundation of the Talent Game Plan. This plan helps plot the roles on the private human capital to public human capital continuum – where the continuum refers to talent "employed" by the company directly, to talent sourced through "partnerships" from other companies. This allows for a multi-year agile workforce/talent plan that delivers evolving skills requirements. It also allows you to shape your build-buy-partner talent agenda. A build-buy-partner plan

Figure 5.1 Organizational Culture diagram (Thiruvengadam, 2020).

should not be built in isolation. It needs to take into consideration the pace of transformation, the speed at which skill requirements shift, the shape of the talent marketplace (availability of talent), and the internal ability to develop talent.

Acquisition of external talent is informed by the talent agenda with a focus on bridging capability gaps and needs. Learning strategy becomes an important lever for transformation, building capabilities, and shaping the culture. Having a clear view of the agency over learning is important to realizing the talent agenda, be it upskilling, reskilling, or out-skilling. These components result in an agile workforce plan that delivers agile organizational evolution, and fluid transformation.

With the confluence of events in the recent past, environmental, social, geopolitical, health and well-being to name a few, companies are grappling with their ability to successfully navigate in the "new order." Technology has played a critical role in how we work over the past 18–24 months. Transformation has become essential for company survival.

Resilience has always been an underlying aspect of transformational change. However, recently, it has come to the forefront. If you step back and think through the organizational inventory process I have outlined in this essay, it primarily addresses organizational resilience. However, we cannot forget the human equation: individual, team, and leadership resilience.

The unspoken nuance of resilience is the well-being of individuals, teams, and leadership. Well-being has been complicated by return-to-work, hybrid work, and virtual work patterns. While we are all new to these new emerging work models, let us accept that we need to learn and evolve. Incorporating this mindset and skillset into the transformation playbook is non-negotiable.

Three Things to Know or Do About Transformational Change

1. Leverage the time-tested approach to inventorying the organization on each dimension.
2. Determine capability needs, translating them into skills requirements; include resilience skills relevant to your company, assess talent, and have a plan to bridge the gaps and needs.
3. Engage the entire organization in the transformation.

Notes

1. John Boudreau and Jonathan Donner, Review of "Are You Ready to Lead Work without Jobs?" *Sloan Management Review*, April 2021, https://shop.sloanreview.mit.edu/store/are-you-ready-to-manage-work-without-jobs.
2. Ravin Jesuthasan and John Boudreau, "Work Without Jobs," *MIT Sloan Management Review*, January 5, 2021, https://sloanreview.mit.edu/article/work-without-jobs/, [August 9, 2021].
3. Ravin Jesuthasan and John W. Boudreau, *Reinventing Jobs* (Brighton: Harvard Business Review Press, 2018).
4. Robert Goffee and Gareth Jones, "Why Should Anyone Be Led by You? What It Takes to Be an Authentic Leader," *Harvard Business Review* (September–October 2000): 63–70.
5. https://futureworkplace.com/ebooks/2021-hr-sentiment-survey/, [August 30, 2021], 6.
6. Ronald Heifetz, Alexander Grashow, and Marty Linsky, *Adaptive Leadership* (Boston: Harvard Business Press, 2009), 7.

7. Heifetz, Grashow, and Linsky, *Adaptive Leadership*, 19.
8. Robert E. Quinn, *Deep Change* (San Francisco: Jossey-Bass, 1996), 203.
9. Quinn, *Deep Change*, 3.
10. Robert Kegan and Lisa Laskow Lahey, *Immunity to Change: How to Overcome It and Unlock Potential in Yourself and Your Organization* (Boston: Harvard Business Press, 2009), 49.
11. Robert Jake Jacobs, *Leverage Change* (Oakland: Berrett-Koehler, 2021), 28–41.
12. Susan Schmitt Winchester and Martha I. Finney, *Healing at Work.* (Dublin: Telemachus, 2021).
13. www.cdc.gov/violenceprevention/aces/about.html, [March 26, 2019].
14. Heather McGhee, *The Sum of Us: What Racism Costs Everyone and How We Can Prosper Together* (New York: One World, 2021).
15. Amy Edmonson, "Psychological Safety and Learning Behavior in Work Teams," *Administrative Science Quarterly* 44, no. 2 (June 1999): 350–383.
16. Karen Jaw-Madson, *Culture Your Culture: Innovating Experiences @ Work* (Bingley: Emerald Publishing, 2018).
17. Gary Hamel, *What Matters Now: How to Win in a World of Relentless Change, Ferocious Competition, and Unstoppable Innovation* (San Francisco: Jossey-Bass, 2012).
18. www.mckinsey.com/featured-insights/leadership/changing-change-management, [September 14, 2021].
19. Robin Speculand, *Excellence in Execution: How to Implement Your Strategy* (New York: Morgan James, 2017), 23.
20. Michael E. Porter, *Competitive Advantage: Creating and Sustaining Superior Performance* (New York: Free Press, 1985).
21. Arnold Mindell, *The Quantum Mind: Journey to the Edge of Psychology and Physics* (Portland: Deep Democracy Exchange, 2012).
22. Roger Connors and Tom Smith, *Journey to the Emerald City: Achieve a Competitive Edge by Creating a Culture of Accountability* (Paramus: Prentice Hall Press, 1999).
23. Faith Fuller and Marita Fridjhon, *Organizational and Relationship Systems Coaching (ORSC™),* 2007, https://crrglobal.com/about/orsc/, [September 9, 2021].
24. Suraj Srinivasan, Jonah S. Goldberg, and Joseph A. Paul, *A Cultural Transformation at Southeastern Grocers* (Boston: Harvard Business School, 2021).
25. The company and individual employee names are fictionalized.
26. www.humansynergistics.com/change-solutions/change-solutions-for-organizations/assessments-for-organizations/organization-culture-inventory, [September 14, 2021].
27. www.themyersbriggs.com/en-US/Products-and-Services/TKI, [September 14, 2021].

Leadership Storytelling (Interviews) – Do Something

In the immediately preceding section of the book, we addressed expert perspectives on leading transformational change via 25 essays; Collective Wisdom as we referred to it. Here in this section, we will take an even deeper dive into leading transformational change. A handful of our Consortium for Change (C4C) members interviewed eight CEOs and other senior business leaders about what it takes to actually *lead* transformational change. These highly experienced executives did not theorize, speculate, or equivocate. They knew it was time to *do* something.

In today's world, where a heightened sense of security often leads to the reminder, "if you see something, say something," these leaders went a step beyond. They each saw something in their organizations that suggested or demanded the need for large-scale transformational change. Not only did they say something about it, but they also did something about it. That is leadership.

The stories you are about to read traverse a wide range of businesses, industries, and circumstances. The settings include energy, entertainment, financial services, retail, and others – and include large, medium, and small revenues and workforces. Yet, every case example called for significant transformational change and highlighted the need for leaders who not only saw or anticipated the need but knew what to do. They took action.

These leaders did not act alone, but they did lead. They each entered the scene in "the middle of the movie." They inherited circumstances, facts, and history that preceded them. They needed to figure out what was going on. And, they knew it was time to lead transformational change.

Our eight leaders set a new vision, mission, or sense of purpose. They drove culture change and innovation. They built a new team, insisted on collaboration, and held people accountable. They globalized, sped things up, communicated more transparently, made people feel like owners, and recognized change champions.

These leaders understood the holistic view of transformational change, built trust, embraced VUCA (Volatility, Uncertainty, Complexity, Ambiguity),

DOI: 10.4324/9781003227137-10

took risks, learned from failures, and delivered results. They treated customers, employees, investors, and communities like they mattered.

Every leader did not do all these things, and certainly not in equal measure. But, they did prioritize what mattered most, relative to the situations they and their organizations were facing. And, they learned – both from what they did and did not do. Now, it is your turn to benefit from those lessons learned. To help you sort out what matters most, each story ends with **Three Things to Know or Do About Transformational Change**, just as we provided in the previous section of the book that includes 25 essays.

Chapter 6

Leaders Lead

Transformational Leadership: Focus on People and Culture

By Barbara Frankel

When Bob Schimmenti was promoted to Senior Vice President of Electric Operations for Con Edison in New York, he recognized that evolving the culture and improving employee engagement was key to the future for the 4,000+ person organization. The industry was changing with an increased focus on safety, affordability for customers while enhancing the customer experience, new business models with clean energy taking center stage, and increased pressure on reliability and resiliency performance. For Bob, people and culture were the foundational elements of transformation that needed to be right to meet the challenges. These priorities became very clear as I began my original work with Bob, and conducted this interview with him.

During our executive onboarding coaching engagement, Bob envisioned the organization transforming from a top-down transactional culture to "a culture of ownership where people know they are valued and respected."

From day one in the new leadership role, Bob made personal changes that signaled employees would be the priority of his leadership style. His office was set up to look more like a living room with sofa and chairs, to encourage dialogue rather than presentations. It became a safe place where anyone in the company could feel comfortable to stop by, and those conversations were typically centered on the individual. He freed up time and eliminated unnecessary meetings to focus on what was most important: the people. Bob committed a significant portion of his time to mentoring, sponsorship, and career development.

Designing, building, operating, and maintaining the energy system and ensuring safety and system performance are critically important in the utility industry. As a leader, Bob said, "the more employees feel connected to a sense

DOI: 10.4324/9781003227137-11

of purpose, the safer they are, the more creative and innovative they are, and the more results the company achieves."

Transforming Leadership Style While Transforming Culture

For Bob, developing a culture where all employees feel included, engaged, and valued is critical to the company's continued success. This was the precursor for building a diverse team and unlocking the potential in all. He knew he needed to transform his own leadership style and trust his team by releasing control. He then set out to build a diverse leadership team.

Bob built an experiential learning process where those closest to the work felt empowered to innovate and solve issues through a collaborative approach. While doing that, he ensured that others understood the value of diversity: diversity of team, thought, and perspective became the value proposition.

As the team embraced this new approach to people and culture, the results followed. His team has delivered top quartile safety performance and recently received the AEIC (Association of Edison Illuminating Companies) safety achievement award. His department was also recognized by J.D. Power as leaders in the customer experience space, with new technology platforms and processes that deliver value to customers each and every day. This success was also reinforced through an annual employee engagement survey that placed his organization among top-performing US companies in safety, employee engagement, alignment, and agility.

Bob's Four-Step Process for Transformational Change

Over the years, Bob has managed many change initiatives and has developed a very simple four-step process in leading change initiatives:

1. Create a Vision
2. Communicate and Gain Acceptance
3. Reinforce and Support
4. Foster Ownership at the Local Levels

Step 1: Create a vision and form a capstone project initiative. Bob spent many hours developing his vision to transform the culture and place employees at the center. He steered a very structured process that started with capstone projects. The capstone project initiative was critical for communicating the vision. Cross-departmental teams working on key business initiatives used experiential learning to demonstrate the vision for the new future and to encourage new ideas. The team input was the start of the appreciation of diversity and more importantly, the importance of value and respect for each other.

Step 2: Use sponsors to communicate and gain acceptance of the vision. He strategically assigned his leadership team to sponsor key focus areas: safety, diversity and inclusion, customer experience, business cost optimization, strategic career development and sponsorship, and operational excellence (resiliency). These leaders acted as advocates in the early phase of the change process and alignment was essential during this step.

Step 3: Reinforce and support the changes by sticking to the plan. This was the area where Bob spent most of his time, as it was the most challenging. Drift is typical as the operational issues of the day compete with the need to practice a new way of learning and collaborating. It is hard to unlearn old ways and stay focused on the foundational culture change initiatives where the people issues need to be elevated. This issue required some deep leadership coaching and periodic pauses on the cascade of the change initiative through the middle managers.

The key was engaging the middle managers to be on board as they directly manage 80% of the organization. Scheduling formal sessions with the various teams to practice the change efforts and engagement with diverse teams was essential to maintain momentum.

Step 4: Train, teach, and engage all leaders. Once there was critical mass connected to the employee empowerment effort, Bob leveraged the middle managers in their role as change agents in the people-centered areas: building diverse teams, recognition, engagement, support, and collaboration.

Bob tied business-related issues into the new approach, so it did not feel incremental to the managers who were already very busy. Dedicated time was carved out in work plan meetings, safety meetings, and then local capstone and engagement initiatives so the team could practice working differently.

The last step proved to be more successful and valuable than expected. Bob assigned culture ambassadors from various levels throughout the organization. These engaged employees provided discretionary effort to support teammates in various business initiatives. This cohort grew to over 40 employees and their dedication and collaboration became the secret sauce for a sustained culture change effort.

Creating Alignment and Identifying Champions

One of the critical efforts that leaders must prioritize is to engage other leaders in aligning with the path forward. Bob had numerous meetings with his peers to align on the needs. He showcased the teams to others and celebrated their accomplishments. He spent endless hours to develop programs, share opportunities, and develop advocacy.

Change happens when you have engaged and inclusive teams, with diversity as the success enabler. This was Bob's focus in introducing and enlisting others around the importance of diversity, inclusion, and engagement. Bob saw things that other people did not see and envisioned a future where the potential of all is unlocked and everyone is valued, respected, and appreciated.

Key Leadership Behaviors and Actions

As a leader, Bob actively demonstrated:

1. Placing people first: He knew it matters how you make people feel.
2. Releasing control so others can learn and be empowered.
3. Modelling the behavior. Starting with yourself as a leader.
4. Creating white space on your calendar to dedicate time for others.
5. Saying no to certain meetings. Staying focused on what is important.
6. Walking around, going into the field often, and connecting with people.
7. Monitoring progress and being visible as a leader.
8. Staying focused on the vision and big picture.
9. Communicating to all team members, "I know you can do this."
10. Planting seeds and asking "what if" questions to mentor and guide staff to come to their own conclusions.
11. Celebrating success.
12. Sending thank you emails once a day and making it personal about someone's contribution to the effort.
13. Focusing on self-improvement.
14. Empowering and inspiring others and cascading the process.

Ensuring Sustainable Culture Change

Bob connected on a regular basis to the teams to ensure that they did not "drift back." He continued to be visible and message on what he wanted. It was a seven-year effort of guiding, messaging, and role modeling on what was important.

He worked with the sponsors of the various initiatives to further encourage ownership. Bob initially assigned four culture ambassadors to carry on the message and suggested that they "bring in a friend." Four culture ambassadors turned into 40 volunteer culture ambassadors over the course of the transformation.

Bob devoted a considerable amount of time onboarding leaders at all levels in the organization. He believes that the culture change will be sustained, as now there is a critical mass that has been involved in creating this culture. Three previous direct reports are on the corporate executive leadership team and will continue to be advocates for diversity, inclusion, and employee engagement.

Three Things to Know or Do About Transformational Change

1. Start with the possibilities you want to see for achieving a leadership vision and results; they will create a future that matters.
2. Communicate, inspire others, and create alignment.
3. Enlist champions who sustain the vision and actions for the future.

What Needs to Be True? Defining the Elements of a Successful Transformational Strategy

By Cheryl Perkins

Throughout her career, Mira Kim has successfully pioneered transformational change in a wide variety of industries. From leading the new business development group at CPG to now being the CEO and owner of American Solar Corporation, Mira has been the driving force behind numerous product launches and acquisitions. In my interview with Mira, we explored what skills a leader needs to develop and implement transformational change successfully, and how to create buy-in with key stakeholders. We also discussed what qualities Mira looks for when building a team and why she believes having fewer resources can fuel transformational change.

During her time at CPG, Mira oversaw several transformational changes that required her to push other executives within the company out of their comfort zones. To begin our conversation, I asked Mira what she believes an organization needs to do to successfully implement transformational innovation.

Mira shared,

> Transformational innovation requires you to explore new spaces, learn new things, and stretch a few of your competencies. At CPG, we implemented a new business development group that was focused on business growth and going after these new spaces in the market. In the beginning, I don't think everyone was fully prepared to understand what transformational change required.

At that time, the company was already a long-established business that was growing, and a lot of company leaders were comfortable continuing with the same processes and trends they had used in the past.

Mira explained,

> Executives wanted more growth, but when it came down to it and we started discussing the new spaces we wanted to pursue, there were a lot of questions because they weren't the same areas that CPG was well known in at that time.

But as the senior director of new business development at CPG, it was Mira's responsibility to push for growth and transformational change. She had to find a way to create buy-in.

"In the beginning, it was about orienting the executive team and making sure we had good support," she explained when discussing her strategy.

> I learned that it's important to carefully prep leaders for what transformational change means and what's required to achieve it. Instead of speaking about transformational change at a high level, we needed to break it down into concrete terms and actionable steps to convey what it meant for the organization. We had to educate from the top down and be resilient throughout our conversations to push for the change we believed in.

And the change Mira believed in was not small. One of the areas her team was focusing on was acquisitions.

She explained,

> We were examining what types of companies CPG typically acquired and where there was room for growth. As a team, we had this saying, "what needs to be true for us to execute a strategy?" To answer that question, we had to go through each piece of our plan at a granular level.

For example, Mira's team had to look at whether it made more sense to acquire premium brands or smaller brands that required more work upfront but had more long-term potential. They also had to define what it meant to acquire high-growth companies and have them flourish. And finally, they had to focus on how they could leverage the best of these small companies and the best of their core competencies to pivot, change, and deliver in a way that was different from their competitors.

"By breaking our strategy down into these granular pieces, we were able to communicate each phase of our plan to the executive team and make sure we were aligned," she noted.

Of course, having these types of conversations with other leaders requires resilience. When I asked Mira what qualities she believes leaders need to display in these challenging situations, she shared that you cannot be someone who fits into a big box, corporate culture perfectly.

"You have to be a bit of a renegade or a rebel to be comfortable working through the ambiguity of the growth process. And if you're unsure where to start, you need to be comfortable asking for advice," she said.

"One of the things I loved about working at CPG was that it was so externally focused. Reaching out to experts to ask questions was just a part of the job," Mira reflected.

> If you're committed to embarking on a transformational change journey, surround yourself with people who have done similar work. Be honest with yourself about what resources and knowledge you need to acquire. Then,

go find the partners, the support, or the mentors you need to weave a quilt of knowledge and experience that you can take with you throughout your journey.

As you are looking for people to surround yourself with, it is also important to consider what qualities and skills you need to create a successful team. After all, it takes a special type of person to have the perseverance to work on transformational change projects.

Mira shared,

> You really have to pick team members who enjoy the work that goes into growing a business. Look for people who love analyzing data and identifying new opportunities. Then select team members who have the core competencies you need and who are willing to broaden their skill set to take on other tasks.

She went on to share that finding team members who are both specialists and generalists is key.

Mira explained,

> For example, you might have someone on your team who specializes in sales, but who is also capable of doing some marketing and helping with financials if you take the time to teach and encourage them. You need functional expertise, but you also need generalists – people who have the mindset for elastic thinking.

At CPG, she worked for a large company but oversaw a team that was small, nimble, and agile. While a lot of companies fail that go big too fast, being small and flexible helped Mira's team adapt to change quickly and implement successful practices. When I asked her what the ideal size is for an innovative team, she shared that change can happen at all levels of an organization, regardless of size, but you have to identify who your key players are.

"You need a small core team that's the heart and soul of driving that change," Mira said. "These are the people that set the tone and the example. They define the principles and the overall vision, but they're also practical."

They know what the end goal is, and they understand what tasks are currently on their priority list.

"When I was at CPG, I had an amazing core team of people who were ready to lead the change. They were really involved in developing both the 'what' and the 'how' of the transformational change process," Mira said.

When other people joined her team later, they noted that everyone there worked differently. With so many tasks to accomplish at such a rapid rate, Mira did not have time to codify everything her team did or how they did it.

"We weren't scheduling a bunch of meetings with each other, we were just adapting and molding ourselves to each new transformational opportunity," she said.

> The team I had was small, but we loved the work we did. There was a camaraderie there and we were confident. It gave us a little sparkle when we presented to external groups, and everyone was so impressed because we were doing things that had never been done before.

In Mira's current role as the CEO and owner of American Solar Corporation, she is exploring new ways to create clean energy through holistic designs that integrate SUNPOWER solar systems, energy storage, estate scale battery backups, and so much more. Everything from her role to the size of her business and the industry she is operating in is very different from CPG, and yet she is continuing to lead transformational change.

She noted,

> I'm taking a lot of the Fortune 500 methods and applying them to this business that my late husband built. We're a high-growth company that's experienced a lot of challenges throughout the pandemic, including supply chain issues. Our sales are lined up, we have dedicated project managers, and it feels good, but we also know we're only hitting a fraction of the market we're capable of.

> Right now, I'm focused on putting the infrastructure in place and defining how we do things so we can scale up.

She also shared that working in construction is much slower than working in consumer-packaged goods, so she has to pace herself and pay close attention to how she titrates resources.

At the same time, Mira knows how to run businesses and build teams, how to prioritize tasks and identify problems. She knows how to ask the question, "what needs to be true for us to execute a strategy?" and help her team embrace that mindset.

"I ask a lot of hypothetical questions, like 'if we were to double your sales, what would we need to do?' Taking the stress out of those conversations is important," she explained. "Even if I'm not committing to that specific goal right now, I need my team to think about what resources we need to get there. It's about establishing the right vocabulary and dialogue."

Of course, operating a small business is also very different from a resources standpoint than working for a large corporation. Yet, Mira believes that working with fewer resources can actually fuel transformative thinking.

"It always inspires me to see how much small companies can accomplish with so few resources. In a way, I think having an excess of resources and money can stifle transformative change because people get too comfortable relying on it," she said.

It is the whole concept of ingenuity by necessity. In the small business world, you cannot just borrow money from another business unit if you do not meet a certain goal. You have to work with the resources and funds you have available.

"When I was at CPG, I was displaced from working in a big business unit with a ton of resources to leading the new business development group, so I saw how resources impact transformational innovation early on in my career," Mira reflected.

In that role, she was interacting with small businesses that were tiny compared to CPG and she was amazed to see what they were doing.

"I really believe that implementing lean budgets can make your team stronger and fuel creativity. Make sure your team has enough money, but don't overspend," she advised. "Make them figure out how they're going to get from point A to B with the budget they have. It can be done! Doing more with less and being comfortable with that ambiguity can really drive transformational change."

Three Things to Know or Do About Transformational Change

1. *Identify your needs*: When you embark on a transformational change journey, it is crucial to break your end goal into small, attainable pieces and identify the resources you need to get there. Ask yourself Mira's question, "what needs to be true for us to execute this strategy?"
2. *Develop a core team with the right skills*: Establishing an inner circle and a cross-functional element, so people can flex in and out, is essential. Look for experts that have the capacity to pivot and take on different roles.
3. *Be comfortable with ambiguity*: Embrace the growth process and let go of the fear of not knowing. Surround yourself with experts who you can learn from and use your creativity to mold your organization or product into what your consumers need.

A Transformational Journey: How CleanWell Reinvigorated Their Entire Company and Flourished Amidst a Pandemic

By Cheryl Perkins

Over the years, CleanWell, a company that produces plant-based, botanical disinfectants and cleaning products, has undergone numerous transformational changes under the leadership of Peter Resnik, Chairman and Owner. In 2016, Stew Lawrence took over as CEO and has been a driving force in transforming everything from the products they sell to the internal organizational processes they follow. A significant part of CleanWell's transformational change also came in the form of branding and package design.

In my interview with Stew, we explored how CleanWell's dedication to their partners, their people, and their customers helped them become such a beloved brand today, and prepared them to flourish in the face of a pandemic. Stew also shared his thoughts on what leaders need to consider before embarking on this type of transformational journey.

To begin our conversation, I asked Stew to tell me what transformational innovation means to him based on his experience transforming the products, branding, and business operations at CleanWell. He explained that while the terms seem almost redundant when paired together, there is a subtle difference.

"Transformational innovation isn't just change for the sake of change," he said. "There's a specific reason and objective associated with it that requires an organization to create something new or change the trajectory of a product, a company, or department at some level."

Recognizing when significant changes need to happen has always been one of Stew's strengths, but when he first stepped into his role as the CEO of Clean-Well he also took the time to really understand the company. While we often hear about the importance of having a 90-day or a 100-day plan, it is also easy for leaders to get swept up in making significant changes as soon as they take on a new role. When I asked Stew about his approach to transformational change, he pointed out that listening is critical.

"A lot of times when we step into a new company, we've already been given a certain objective to work toward or we get placed on a path that's been predetermined. It's important to take the time to pause, listen, and understand those objectives," he said.

That pause and listen piece really is critical. Taking the time to understand what our organizations and colleagues need from us can help us make smarter decisions that lead to long-term success, but true transformational change also requires us to listen to our customers and consumers.

"At the end of the day, all transformational and innovative changes come down to the consumer in one way or another," Stew pointed out. "That's something I made sure my team at CleanWell was aware of."

He also shared that at other companies he has worked with, teams needed to completely restage brands that did not quite resonate with consumers the first time they were launched.

> In those instances, we paid close attention to consumer insights so we could make changes to the brand name, color scheme, packaging, and personality of the brand to meet their needs. It's a process. Sometimes these changes work right away and sometimes it takes more research. Insights may look good on paper, but consumers can be tricky, so it takes a mindset of continuous improvement to be able to tap into the right target market.

At CleanWell, Stew knew that the backstory of the company was important. Consumers today want to know more about the companies they choose to support and the people who work there. He also understood that any changes they made as an organization, even if they were from an operational or a cost standpoint, needed to flow down to their consumers in a way that was economically feasible.

While transformational change can certainly happen in the back office if it involves operational processes or internal culture, transformational change that is consumer-facing really focuses on impacting the consumers' behavior. As Stew pointed out, your goal is either to get them to try your product or repeat their purchase.

"In the trial phase, your goal is to influence consumers' willingness or ability to try your product or service. You might be conducting research, testing out different price points, or trying different marketing techniques to figure out what entices them," he explained.

> After you get consumers to try your product, your goal is to get them to repeat that behavior. There are a lot of companies that are really good at getting consumers to try a product by offering it for free or at discounted rates, but building brand loyalty can be more challenging. For example, I would love to drive a Ferrari for free. That's fun, but if I suddenly have to pay full price for it, I might decide to reconsider.

Of course, the type of transformational change that impacts consumer behavior takes a lot of courage to implement. This type of change does not simply happen overnight.

"It takes a lot of patience, even when it feels like you might not have the time to be patient. Any opportunity you have to take a deep breath, stop and think, and maybe even wait can pay off in dividends," Stew explained.

And on the flip side, leading transformational change requires you to take risks. Not every decision is going to be a good one, but as leaders, we have to move forward to drive innovation.

"I've probably learned more from the things I've done wrong in my career than from the things I've done right – and that's okay as long as you have the proper mindset. You just have to hope the good decisions outweigh the bad ones and that the bad ones aren't too bad," Stew shared.

One way to build this resilience and the ability to take risks is to surround yourself with the right people. When I asked Stew what qualities he looks for when building a team, he noted that trust and transparency are critical.

"Having trust with your team internally is a lot like a marriage. If you don't have trust inside the four walls of your home, then you have some stuff to work on," he explained.

> You can't please everyone all the time, but you need team members who see value in your organization, believe in you as a person, and have faith in what you stand for. There are going to be times when you trip over yourself as a leader, but having a team that acknowledges you're human and is still committed to you for the long-term is critical.

In addition to having a strong foundation of trust internally, Stew has worked to build trust and understanding with CleanWell's partners. While sharing a common vision is essential, some of the other qualities he looks for when determining whether to enter into a partnership include the willingness to listen and be flexible. That flexibility became increasingly important throughout the pandemic when supply chain issues changed operations for many businesses.

Stew said,

> During the pandemic, we had to have a tough conversation with one of our vendors about how it wasn't feasible for us to continue to live by the agreement we originally established with them. We also knew that we didn't have a force majeure and we didn't want to make the situation litigious. So, we asked our partner to help us help them and vice versa. We still wanted to find a way to establish a new agreement that benefited their team.
>
> In the end, we worked out a different compensation structure with this partner during the pandemic instead of simply canceling the partnership altogether, which they appreciated. On their end, they were a great partner because they were willing to listen and be flexible with our arrangement.

That type of thoughtfulness and real human connection is something Stew strives to find in all of CleanWell's partners. Despite all of the challenges the pandemic brought with it, CleanWell actually saw an increase in sales during this time. Stew attributed this success to the way the entire company came together and their dedication to maintaining those strong relationships with their brand partners.

Stew explained,

> Everyone understood that this was a once-in-a-lifetime event, and we really felt like – because we were producing disinfectants – we owed it to our brand partners to do as much as we could for them so they could get our products in the hands of consumers. But, it was even deeper than that.

His team was seeing all of the different places they could have a positive impact firsthand.

"I had a friend that came up to me after our kids' hockey practice and his navy blazer was completely bleached on the ends," Stew shared.

> He explained that he had to wipe down the service center he worked at with bleach in between every person that came in for training, which was multiple times a day. All of his clothes were falling apart and his hands were torn up because of this. That was a lightbulb moment for me when I realized CleanWell produces a disinfectant that doesn't use harsh chemicals, so it doesn't affect people's skin. As a company, we really started to see the impact we could have on consumers and how we could improve their lives.

Throughout the pandemic, we have all experienced challenges we never thought we would face, but as leaders, we certainly had an extra level of responsibility to our teams, our partners, our customers, and our consumers. Looking back at his experiences throughout the pandemic, Stew notes that many of CleanWell's competitors were too eager to make a profit, which has backfired on them in several ways.

"They cut a lot of corners and made promises they couldn't keep, which resulted in some pretty massive lawsuits. At CleanWell, we were really patient with our approach," Stew noted. "We realized that even the pandemic would eventually pass, and it was important for us to be loyal to our partners, our consumers, and each other. You have to take care of those who take care of you."

Three Things to Know or Do About Transformational Change

1. *Listen to understand:* Take the time to listen to other people in your organization as well as your partners and your consumers. The more you understand the reasons behind their objectives and needs, the better equipped you will be to create transformational change that serves them.

2. *Take calculated risks:* Be patient, but do not be afraid to take risks. Use the insights and research you have available and continue optimizing your products, services, and processes until you get it right.

3. *Be loyal:* Surround yourself with people who are honest and transparent. Respect the relationships you have built with vendors, colleagues, employees, and your consumers by being loyal to them.

Finding Relevance

By Patrick R. Powaser, Ph.D.

As a new CEO, Monica Belz came into the role ready to make a change. A natural disaster took her in a different direction and opened doors for Monica's organization to find its purpose, its relevance. She now finds balance between the financials and the impact Kaua'i Government Employees Federal Credit Union has on the community in which it operates.

"Someone different!" was the unanimous response when I asked the Kaua'i Government Employees Federal Credit Union (KGEFCU) Board whether they were looking for a clone or someone different to succeed the retiring CEO. The retiring CEO chimed in with her support for change as well. "I've taken it as far as I can. We need someone else, someone different to take it to the next level," she added.

Enter Monica Belz, a 30-something-year-old rock climbing, free diving, snowboarding millennial who took over as CEO of the then 70-year-old Credit Union (CU) in January 2018. The Board said they wanted change, and Monica, along with Mother Nature, delivered.

Sharing Vision, Building the Team

Monica knew she needed a strong team to get the KGEFCU to wherever it was they were headed. She searched for and recruited executive team members who did not think like her and who had different backgrounds and experiences than she did. In doing so, she was also scanning the horizon toward an unknown future with an eye on building the capacity and resiliency needed to be successful as the business environment and community needs changed.

Even with a powerful vision and a strong team, Monica faced challenges in pinning down the organization's purpose and its continuing relevance in the community. She has compared the CU to a World War II-era rusty tank (KGEFCU was founded in 1947) trying to do the work of a drone in a modern combat zone.

As her executive coach during her first year at the helm, I worked with Monica to map out where she wanted to go and how to best rely on her A-team to plot the course to get there. She took a step back from relying on the CU's historical brand and operational history and focused on the customer by employing ethnographic research to understand what the members of the CU needed (Credit Unions are member-owned nonprofits). She soon was gifted a tremendous amount of ethnographic data from an unanticipated, unforgiving, and unwanted source.

Finding Community

On April 14, 2018, it started raining on Kaua'i, especially over the island's North Shore. In the next 24 hours, some locations had received over 50 inches of rain, breaking national rainfall records.

The course of the Hanalei River was changed. Houses floated out to sea. Landslides wiped out roads and effectively cut off much of the North Shore from the rest of the island. Residents suddenly had nowhere to live, no jobs, and no access to the rest of the island and its services, including gasoline, electricity, food, financial resources, and clean water.

KGEFCU immediately created a new "Disaster Loan" product to help North Shore residents, most of whom were not KGEFCU members. But they *were* members of the community. Monica and her team had found their purpose.

Monica's well-honed crisis management skills kicked in to respond to the flooding. She had been honing those abilities most of her life responding to disasters around the globe, building on the skills she first learned as a wildland firefighter starting at age 14. "In times of crisis, the rules get thrown out the window and the focus shifts to taking care of those in need," she shared. Staff, executives, and the Board all aligned with what needed to happen and the role the KGEFCU could and should serve.

Adorned with black KGEFCU t-shirts, the team showed up to help, providing fuel, food, water, and clothing. North Shore residents initially reacted with "Who the heck is this organization?" As the only financial institution on-scene, and a small one at that, many residents did not know KGEFCU existed. The team quickly became known as the "Black Angels." Getting financial resources to those in need was a challenge with the roads literally swept out into the ocean. Boats, jet skis, and swimming proved to be the transportation methods of choice. Carrying drybags loaded with communications and financial resources, the team literally jumped in feet first and made their way to shore and to a community in need.

A New Focus on the Business

As the chaos of the floods began to settle, the team could get back to reinventing itself and the CU. Monica had studied change in her MBA program at the Thunderbird School of Global Management but realized that it is very different when you are in the middle of it. She had seen firsthand that change can be a physiological and psychological stressor, akin to trauma. She knew it was her responsibility to change the CU but did not want that change to lead to trauma for the team, members, Board, or community.

As we worked together on what the change would look like, I introduced the team to Sundance Consulting's change model[1] which focuses on three key dimensions:

- **Strategic Vision** (*Why* change?)
- **Change** (specifically, *What* is changing?)
- **Transition** (how will the change impact those involved – the *Who?*)

We focused a lot of energy on the Transition piece to understand how changing the CU would impact the minds, hearts, and souls of those involved.

Understanding those emotions and reactions provided valuable input in crafting the organizational culture that would be needed to support the new CU and meet the needs of all stakeholders.

Change for Good

Monica and her team quickly realized that the culture of KGEFCU needed to change to fit with the community-based organization it had become. While the CU was member-owned, it was still a financial institution with all the Federal and State regulation that goes with it. Over the years, the regulatory burden had created a mentality of excessive risk intolerance, focus on process, and conservatism. Those are all good characteristics for an organization that is safeguarding your wealth. However, taken to an extreme, an organization's culture can become focused on excessive compliance, generating fear of mistakes, arduous processes, and burdensome rules. Interactions with customers and meaningful impact on the community suffers.

With the CU's newfound identity as a core pillar of the community, balancing safety and compliance with caring and relationship building became a priority. Staff were encouraged to learn more about each member and build deeper relationships. The team could then serve the true needs of the community versus engaging in a simple, quick transaction. The senior team had to shift their efforts as well to support the staff's new behaviors, adjust performance metrics, and model community-focused behaviors more effectively.

When the Board hired Monica, they had emphasized the need for change. And then got more change than they had ever imagined. This was a time of reflection, stress, and learning for the Board as well. Monica operated differently than her predecessor. She brought her senior team to Board meetings with her and encouraged them to participate when their expertise would contribute to the meetings. The Board saw itself evolve from being change-averse to tolerating and even celebrating being uncomfortable with change.

During the rain and flooding in 2018, the need for a community-based financial institution located on the North Shore quickly became clear. Part of KGEFCU's growth strategy and community focus was to open the first CU on that part of the island. In 2020, KGEFCU's North Shore branch opened to serve the needs of a long-underserved part of the community. In turn, the CU gained greater visibility in the community and across the island.

Doors Open

In the Fall of 2020 Monica was named Hawai'i's "Business Executive of the Year."[2] KGEFCU was also designated as a Community Development Financial Institution (CDFI) by the US Department of the Treasury, one of only five in Hawai'i. While Monica may downplay those accomplishments personally, she revels in how those designations open doors, create exposure, and generate opportunities to have deeper conversations with members and the community.

When COVID-19 hit, the CDFI designation allowed KGEFCU to be a significant funnel of federal financial assistance into the community. Being able to provide support once again to businesses and community members who most needed it fit well with the CU's new identity.

Today, Monica regularly looks beyond her organization and sees the value of all CUs on the island and across the state banding together for the benefit of their communities. Whether CU members or not, each individual is an important contributor to the community.

Daily, KGEFCU ensures it remains relevant and connected with the community.

Monica has reflected on her tenure so far as CEO of KGEFCU and all that has happened over the past few years. She shared a few things that were key to the successful change at the CU. Collaborating with stakeholders including the Board, staff, and community was key. Staying the course as a leader means not quitting when things get exceptionally tough, you just keep going. Other important success factors include learning from mistakes, building a strong team, and finding purpose.

Through my lens as a coach and consultant, having a client who was willing to explore new ideas and behaviors, build a strong team around her, step back and question why her organization really exists, and grow KGEFCU into something bigger than itself was a gift.

Three Things to Know or Do About Transformational Change

1. Learn from failures and celebrate the small successes.
2. Build a stellar team that can go well beyond what you can do individually and beyond the organization's current size and complexity.
3. Find a bigger, higher purpose: your relevance.

Cultural Transformation: Linking Leadership Behavior to Positive Results

By Susan Robertson

A positive and cohesive culture is the key to unlocking talent, potential, happiness, and engagement in the workplace. As Peter Drucker says, "Culture eats strategy for breakfast!" Without a powerful and collaborative culture your team cannot create a purpose, strategy, or plan that aligns values and behaviors with organizational goals.

Tommie English, a Senior Vice President and Executive Director at a Fortune 100 Financial Services Company, led a team of over 1,000 people. I interviewed her to get her perspective on priority actions and lessons learned from the cultural transformation she led.

Not long ago, Tommie and her organization were immersed in a "drill and kill" culture. Executive leadership, despite revenue and scorecard successes, would drill down on less relevant details until they found a mistake or a question that could not be answered. This created a hostile, fear-based, command and control culture where teamwork, agility, and adaptability did not exist. No matter how much performance improved, it was never enough.

Despite low employee engagement scores and high attrition rates, leadership refused to change their tactics, and results began to plummet. Change was needed.

When Good People Work in Bad Cultures

Everyone on Tommie's team did what they had to do to survive. The senior leaders in Tommie's division devised a disciplinary system that escalated in severity for managers who were not meeting their Key Performance Indicators. The goal was to scare and shame employees into working harder to exceed organizational goals.

This tactic worked. Everyone on Tommie's team was scared and out for themselves. Some employees experienced physical illnesses; others left the company.

To survive in this environment, Tommie ensured her team not only met their goals but exceeded them. There were five customer service centers worldwide, and when compared to her peers, her scorecard was best-in-class. Although her employees were fundamentally unhappy, they were motivated by this performance success and were known to brag about their perfect scorecards, perpetuating the competitive culture.

"Don't get me wrong, I am competitive, and I like to be the best in class, but it is equally important to lead from the heart," said Tommie. In the current culture, there was no tolerance for Tommie to experiment with a compassionate leadership style. She had lost her sense of self while immersed in a culture where there was no room for error, creativity, or agility.

Tommie added,

> Under the old leadership of "drill and kill," I had to learn to communicate a compelling message that did not align with my values. I would be honest with my employees, however, we had a job to do. We all had our different reasons for staying, such as needing the paycheck, love for the people, and wanting to come out as a victor in spite of the situation.

At last, the team was afforded the opportunity to provide anonymous feedback via an employee opinion survey – the catalyst sparking change. Worldwide, the results were resoundingly clear and executive leadership became acutely aware of the destructive fear-based culture pervasive in their company. The executive leadership team took action to improve cultural dynamics and brought in a new head of operations to instigate change.

Insight and Courage: The First Step in Cultural Change

Under new leadership, Tommie was encouraged to look deeply into the culture of her team.

Her first step was to be courageous and gain insights with detailed feedback from her team. Tommie knew it would not be easy to receive all of the feedback, and that after hearing it, she would be obligated to act on it.

The operations executive team contracted me, Susan Robertson, to work with Tommie's team. We created a leadership and cultural transformation roadmap and interviewed and surveyed over 325 people in the company. After analyzing the data, we conducted a two-day team session where Tommie and her peers explored their leadership behavior, team dynamic, and cultural effectiveness. She learned that despite working against it, she had indeed adopted some of the "drill and kill" culture within her organization.

Tommie said,

> When Susan started working with us, the whole team was in disarray. We had just received the results of our Employee Opinion Survey. Our results were horrible. People were afraid of losing their jobs. We were stressed out, scrambling everyday just to survive. When we got our executive report and individual feedback, it was like reading a horror story. But it was out there and it was from that point that we started to do the work to create a better environment. Of course, we had to start with our own self-awareness.

Tommie acknowledged to me,

> We were very competitive. We had to admit that we didn't collaborate with
> the other teams, and that was shocking to me. [We learned] that we didn't
> share best practices. That we had a secret sauce, and we were not telling
> people what the secret was. That was the biggest feedback that came from
> outside of our team [and] within our team, it just screamed really loud.

She learned that by not sharing her best practices for performance success with
her peers, her team became insular. She was perceived as a non-team player
within the company. These insights motivated Tommie to begin the culture
change process. She knew she had to start with herself and change her own
leadership behaviors.

Clarity: The Second Step in Cultural Performance

We worked fervently to assess the employee voice and understand how leadership behaviors and culture impacted her overall results. We completed employee
sentiment and climate interview processes, gathered 360° behavioral information on the top leaders in the center, and with this data in hand Tommie and
her team were courageous to review the results. We quickly identified issues
with internal competition, silo-building, infighting, and lack of teamwork. The
team was able to define three major gaps in their leadership and teamwork
behaviors that adversely impacted the culture and climate.

With newfound clarity, Tommie and her team shared the three major gaps
they had identified with the entire center, promptly followed by a promise to
take action and create positive change. They wanted all the employees to know
they were heard. And equally as important, that they are now accountable for
making the right changes for improvement. Each leader then shared their cultural and climate findings with their organization, along with their leadership
action plans for change.

This type of open communication was novel and generated a new baseline of
trust and excitement that things would be different.

Mutual Respect: An Imperative Component to
Adopting Cultural Change

A key element identified by the team was the lack of respect for differences in
leadership style and opinion. Two of Tommie's strongest leaders had opposing
leadership approaches and did not respect each other, ultimately leading to the
biggest impact on culture. Working with Tommie and her direct reports in a
two-day session, we learned the team had developed workarounds to avoid
infighting, which cost the team in terms of efficiency and effectiveness.

Using personality assessments, the team dove deeper into understanding awareness and emotional intelligence. We focused on issues of control and the need to be right. The team bravely faced their personal issues of leadership control and understood how the need to control and the need to be right often led to disrespect.

They decided to set aside their differences and created respectful ways to work through disagreement and conflict. The team was encouraged by the possibility that focusing on the people side of the business could help them realize even better processes and increase performance. We conducted assessments and adopted a cultural roadmap that later became what is now called the REAL Results Model, which theorizes that focusing on people dynamics and process improvement results in performance:

The REAL Results Model™:
People + Process = Performance[3]

Under the prior "drill and kill" culture, Tommie and her team primarily focused on process improvement while pushing people to make their numbers. When the team added the people focus and teamwork side of the equation, their performance dramatically improved.

Buy-In: The Third Step in Cultural Effectiveness

With their newfound respect and ability to work through tough conflict together, the team took the next step to create shared goals and obtain buy-in from every participant. To help the team move forward, they employed the Effectiveness Factor Equation™:

Idea Level × Participant Buy-In = Effectiveness Level
10-Level Idea × 0 Buy-In = 0 or Low Effectiveness
5-Level Idea × 5 Buy-In = 25 Increased Effectiveness
7-Level Idea × 7 Buy-In = 49 Higher Effectiveness and Performance

Barry Robertson, creator of The Effectiveness Factor Equation™ emphasizes that to improve effectiveness and productivity, "leaders need to give up the need to be right for the desire to be effective." Individuals and teams can have a 10-Level Idea, the greatest idea that ever existed, but without buy-in the idea never grows legs. When all team members help generate an idea, they have increased Buy-In, which improves Effectiveness and Performance.[4]

Tommie's team moved away from individual success measures and developed shared leadership, team, and culture-focused goals directly correlated with their KPIs and scorecard goals. They willingly opened themselves to listening to ideas from everyone within the center.

Tommie shared,

> One of my mantras was "change is good . . . if it produces positive results."
> My team adopted this mantra as we worked to change perceptions, increase
> team dynamics, and increase overall performance. We also adopted the slo-
> gan, "duty before complaint."

Celebrate Change: The Fourth Step in Cultural Transformation

As Tommie developed her "love them or I'll lose them" style of leadership,
she and her team began to find and track positives and celebrate movement
forward. They still addressed the areas where development was needed, but
intentionally spent more time tracking positives. This led to increased employee
engagement and satisfaction, and the staff was inspired to perform better.

When they linked leadership behavior to results, the results dramatically
improved. The average handle time for solving customer issues declined, while
their customer satisfaction scores increased. Employee retention rates improved,
and Tommie's organization reduced expenses 15% year-over-year for the next
three years. They challenged themselves to find new ways of working together
as a team. Consequently, they generated more creativity and agility and started
experimenting with new ways to accomplish similar goals after their shared
experience of success. They credited their shared success to their entire team.

In her reflections about her experience, Tommie relayed, "Even though we
had our dysfunctions as many teams and families do, we were a highly cohesive
team and our work with Susan's organization helped us to realize and embrace
that cohesiveness with more awareness. It was truly transformational."

Three Things to Know or Do About Transformational Change

1. To affect transformational change, you must lead from within, as yourself. Adopting traits of a destructive culture to survive will not serve you
   or your team. Having the courage to lead with your heart, gut, and brain
   will ultimately reflect your true leadership style, inspire others to follow
   suit, and create the change everyone desires.
2. You can create transformational change on your own. You do not need
   to suffer in a toxic environment and wait for a changing of the guard up
   top to infect positive change within your own team. The culture of your
   team depends on you.
3. Positive leadership behaviors and positive team behaviors can tangibly
   improve quantitative and qualitative results for your business.

Leading Transformational Change: An Experiential Shift From Doing to Being

By Adrienne Shoch

The art of transformational change is shifting focus from linear business processes, motivated by doing instead of being, to fluid reorientation driven by people and adaptive behavior.

It is increasingly difficult, as the pace of change accelerates, to trust "we are where we need to be." To know where we are, we find ourselves moving away from lagging Key Performance Indicators (KPIs) and results to real-time experiential data based on relationships and conversations. Knowing the degree to which change is taking root or gaining traction is a sensing exercise in awareness, observation, and listening. As a leader of change, trusting your experience of what is happening is often the data you and your team need to confirm when you are on and off track.

This interview addresses change from the perspective of *The Change Agent*, who meets transformational change as an opportunity for personal and professional growth for themselves and those they lead. What is it about the catalyst who navigates uncharted territory without a compass in search of a true north, without destroying the ship, and leaving legacy intact in service of a better future?

I interviewed Jennifer Guidry, Vice President of Global HSE (Health, Safety, Environmental) and Sustainability at Precision Drilling, to explore the role she plays as *The Change Agent*. Jennifer and I did not discuss a particular change project or initiative. Instead, we explored the overarching role and work of *The Change Agent* – their attunement within a changing system.

During our conversation, Jennifer summed up our shared sentiments as follows,

> I believe you are not a Change Agent unless you understand what makes you a Change Agent. You have to do the work in developing yourself and your capacity to change in all aspects of your life to be a true leader of change. I have come to learn, to lead change, I had to embody and model compassion, empathy, courage, and vulnerability. Without self-work, you cannot embody or foster what change requires.

By its nature, change is fluid, inherent, and systemic. Transformation is not seen or led through a myopic lens of components and static models. Instead, it is viewed through a holistic lens from which dynamic parts integrate and create something more relevant, cohesive, and resilient.

Jennifer explained,

> From the perspective of *The Change Agent*, transformational change is less about what you have to *do* and more about who you have to *be* in order to envision and create a different future for yourself and others. Embodying change requires practice in self-inquiry and reflection.

The ability to change and drive change is inherent to every human being in every moment. Every cell in our body is configured to grow, evolve, and change without thought or interference. So, why is change so disruptive and difficult if we are designed to embody change? Jennifer and I discussed this fundamental question – and the role of *The Change Agent* – using the lenses of Awareness, Culture, and Trust.

Awareness

As Jennifer and I explored building awareness, she surmised,

> Awareness begins with knowing who you are and aligning it with who you want to become. It's a capacity developed through deep self-actualization and a desire to embrace and embody the fear of not knowing. It's the ability to clear away the fear of truly knowing, and accepting yourself as a vessel, or "leader-ship," of change.

Self-awareness requires self-work and commitment. In the chaos of change, tuning into awareness comes from the practice of reflection and inquiry supported by three questions:

1. What skills and behaviors need to be "dialed up," or "dialed down," to bring balance throughout change?
2. What are the blind spots keeping me narrowly focused?
3. What may be getting in the way of me embodying and aligning with this change?

"As *The Change Agent* becomes increasingly aware, there is more focus on what matters; derailers become easier to anticipate and overcome," added Jennifer.

Culture

Jennifer and I agree, there are no more powerful forces shaping change than culture and legacy. These forces operate as accelerators and barriers playing a pivotal role in building momentum and trust. Legacy, in particular, plays a large role in anchoring us in the past, especially when uncertainty prevails and changing direction feels unclear and unsafe.

The Change Agent understands the power of this tension and connects the importance of legacy to the present and future in a *Timeline Map*.

Timeline Maps visualize the dynamics of change and bring them to life in real-time. From the Map, milestones, events, and patterns are highlighted to show how the system continues to evolve. It serves as a guide to the future and portrays how events build on one another and where they get stuck.

Mapping a unique, iterative process of transformation diminishes the fear of uncertainty and opens up safe access to future possibilities. Here is how it works.

Begin with the inception of the entity (organization, function, team, etc.,) and end with the possibilities of a different future:

- Map out a chronological series of key events, milestones, contributors/contributions that brought you to your current state
- Connect the dots using hard lines to create a visual path from past to present
- Create a new path with dotted lines, and incrementally map out a series of future events, milestones, and contributions leading to successful change

Timeline Maps reveal events that move us in and out of various dimensions of change. They help us relate, connect, and make meaning. In turn, these events illustrate what was required to make change happen:

- What needed to happen to provoke an event?
- What change did the event provoke?
- What was the response?

To take it one step further, *Timeline Mapping* is a powerful guide used to uncover elements that support, derail, or neutralize the work of *The Change Agent*:

- What change or event occurred as a natural progression of evolution?
- What change or event was anticipated or strategically planned?
- What change or event was unexpected and forced reaction?

System dynamics teaches everything has its place and order and moves us to where we are and where we need to go. Everything is connected; change in one part of the system at any given time will impact other parts of the system at any given time.

Trust

Trust is foundational to change, and modeling trust begins with *The Change Agent*. It begins with intuition and is reinforced with creating a sense of safety. *The Change Agent* has a keen sense of what is possible and brings together vision, strategy, and relationships that cut across hierarchy, formal and informal networks, and external forces shaping the environment.

In discussing the role of *The Change Agent*, Jennifer and I concluded that the brain, body, and instincts (i.e., intuition, awareness, and internal intelligence) are used collectively to gauge what is happening internally and externally. Weighing physical sensations that we feel during times of stress against interpretations of data found in information, conversation, and events is a powerful combination that produces real-time data and guidance.

Trusting instincts requires practice in testing assumptions and validating what you do not know or think of as undeniably true. These practices are essential to developing trust and instinct. It does not happen in a vacuum and requires reliance and learning from others. For *The Change Agent*, building communities of trust leading to safety, commitment, and powerful real-time data is mission critical. Agreement is not required . . . listening, observing, and trust building are!

Cultivating trust is an intentional process that requires commitment. If you lose it, it is not easy to recover. Humans have a highly active and accurate internal "threat" radar which is activated by uncertainty. The brain thrives on certainty. Amid uncertainty, there is no trust. It is a bio-physiological response that is a barrier to change.

As *The Change Agent*, you know how well you are doing when you sense what is happening inside and around you. From Jennifer's experience,

> It's in the gut. You can feel it, hear it, and see it. The first notable shift comes in the quality of conversation and the stories people tell about the past and future. Relationships relax, there is more curiosity and listening involved.

When you pay attention and listen well, you will be surprised at how transparent people are. Transparency is magnified through awareness. There is no better indicator to effectively gauge the performance of change than through the people experiencing it in real time.

Three Things to Know or Do About Transformational Change

1. Transformational change is less about what you have to *do* and more about who you have to *be* to make a difference.
2. A holistic approach to change leverages the power of the past to reorient the present and shape the future.
3. Trusting yourself and what you are experiencing often provides the best data to confirm you are on track.

The Best 30 Minutes in a Family's Day

By David Yudis, Psy.D., MBA

There are roughly 1.9 billion children in the world today. What a better world this would be if we could deliver to each of those children their best 30 minutes of every day. Four hundred Disney Stores around the world transformed to fulfill this inspiring mission.

Without Change, a Strong Start Can Falter

This is a story of inspirational transformation. It begins in 1987 with the launch of the first Disney Store and fast forwards to the year 2004. After rapid expansion and a roller coaster retail ride, The Disney Stores were licensed to The Children's Place in North America and Canada.

If it had gone well, the story might have ended there with another entity essentially managing Disney's brand in vertical retail. In 2007, however, there was a change in leadership at The Children's Place and their Board of Directors decided they were no longer interested in running the license.

This was a tipping point moment. Disney's Board of Directors asked Consumer Products Chairman Andy Mooney to start working on a secret project to determine what to do. Options included licensing the Stores chain to another entity, closing the chain down, or taking the stores back and operating them again from inside.

Be Careful What You Wish for

In 2008, senior leadership made the decision to bring the Stores chain back inside Disney's operations. James Fielding, one of the leaders who worked on the secret project to determine the Stores' fate, was named President of The Disney Stores.

This was a dream job for Mr. Fielding, a position he may have aspired to his entire life, yet he did not know at the time that this would be it. As he reflected on taking the role, what resonates with him now is the saying, "Be careful what you wish for."

As he assembled his team, Jim's mission was to articulate the "why now?" for relaunching The Disney Stores in-house. It could not have happened at a more inopportune time. As late 2008 rolled around, the global financial crisis was in full swing and real estate and financial markets melted down.

To get a taste of what day-to-day life was like working in this space at the time, consider a business experiencing 25%+ revenue decreases, operating in crisis mode, and doing so when consumers were neither shopping nor going to malls.

Given these circumstances, it appeared the business had a short lifeline. Several areas of support, however, made all the difference. First, the senior leadership team at Disney supported the venture even though the numbers did not look good. This was rare and represented leadership's belief that The Disney Stores brand had value beyond financial, to the greater good of the organization. Second, Steve Jobs was one of the members of the Board of Directors at the time. He believed in brands being established in mall-based retail and compared the opportunity to successes achieved with Apple's Retail Stores. Finally, 400 stores in cities around the world provided Disney with another marketing vehicle that had a physical manifestation of what it was like to experience the company's magic.

One Gear: Overdrive and Fun

The transformation went into overdrive and began to work based on two factors. Both were dependent on partnerships with the consumer products division leads for finance and human resources.

The CFO provided consistent capital and investment but did so with oversight that enabled Mr. Fielding's team to manage change in phases. It all began with a unified mission that became "the best 30 minutes of a family's day." That statement spoke to everyone and energized the team while making hard work fun. These values sprung directly from Disney's global culture but were embedded in ways that had never been done before. The team knew that if they could create a safe, clean, exciting, immersive entertainment destination for families, people would visit. The goal was to ensure that when a family crossed the imaginary line from the outside world into a store, they moved past a threshold and into a story that would become the best part of their day. Ultimately, a trip to the Store could be a reward for a good report card, a stopover after school sports, or a brief mini-vacation from the stresses of any day.

The CHRO engaged a talent acquisition, development, and review process to ensure the best and brightest talent were hired and integrated, which helped to turn around results in an overdrive pace. The culture was fast-paced, vibrant, and exciting. Execution followed a playbook of classic Retail 101 but was enveloped by the magic of Disney to manage the brand. Mr. Fielding took guidance from his partners and repeatedly sought to find pearls among his talent, people that he could challenge, stretch, and then elevate to take the business higher.

What made working with The Disney Stores so uplifting also created some of the most challenging obstacles. With the expanse of Disney's reach, there was a multitude of inputs to the Stores business. Suggestions came from every angle of the company and included guidance on product, e-commerce, store design, real estate, strategy, and the overall Store portfolio. Within each of these dimensions were further breakdowns. For example, film property tie-ins as opportunities to create product. Relentlessly, every week, Mr. Fielding and his team were tasked with attacking issues and making decisions. This was gratifying but exhausting. It was quickly apparent that leadership teams needed to be empowered, trusted, and have an aligned sense of the mission, as well as be in charge of how to execute to meet deadlines.

Ironically, strengths overdone can also be weaknesses. Whereas support and reach were aspects of The Walt Disney Company that benefitted The Disney Stores in their transformation, Mr. Fielding also pointed to these areas as specific obstacles that could hinder progression. While retail sold at the company's theme parks was generated by a captive audience, those guests visiting a given park, the Disney Stores were the only business in vertical, stand-alone retail. The Stores had to fight for and provide a compelling reason to generate guest traffic. This meant speaking a different language, the language of retail. On the plus side, the Stores would prototype and do things in their locations that no one else across the Company was doing. On the downside, that required constant communication, influence, and bringing leadership at Corporate along as buy-in was pursued for new ideas.

Licensing in the consumer products division was growing exponentially. Again, while a significant fuel for a strong growth engine, the Stores had to equally produce great product in their vertical chain. That meant competing with oneself. Without disparaging or denigrating licensed product showing up at other retailers, The Disney Stores had to differentiate and still win in their focused categories.

Two Heads Are Better Than One

Unequivocally, when asked what the single most important action is required to effect successful transformation, Mr. Fielding shared that alignment on mission and vision was key. From his leadership team to the field workforce, understanding what the Disney Stores were trying to do, how each individual's role contributed to that effort, and requiring creative thinking and action, ensured that any time an obstacle showed up, the team would persist and work through it. It also helped that throughout the culture, they reinforced the need to bring forth solutions to any problem, not just state or complain about a problem. Mr. Fielding had a philosophy that two heads are better than one and he used this every day. It also reinforced for him that he did not expect to have all the answers.

There was lasting change that accompanied the Stores transformation. From the time the Stores were moved back into internal Disney operations, operating income increased $120 million. The growth of digital shopping, which began with this change, extended to all areas of the organization. Other areas of Disney also benefitted. The Stores became the largest seller of Theme Park tickets besides American Express, were responsible for opening more Disney Visa accounts than anyone else, and also became one of the largest purveyors of DVDs.

Three Things to Know or Do About Transformational Change

1. **Vision–Mission alignment is key.** If they capture what the organization stands for and speak simply to all stakeholders, everything else falls into place.
2. **Senior leadership must be bought in from the start.** Once in motion, active partnering with key senior leaders reinforces successive wins.
3. **Make work fun.** Work may always be work but people do not think of it as such, nor do they feel it when it is fun. When people enjoy what they are doing, asking for discretionary engagement is unnecessary. People willingly go the extra distance to get something done and smile along the way. This commitment leads to growth and development and is infectious across a culture.

Culture Eats Strategy and Then Some: How to Have a Balanced Approach to Driving Transformation

By David Yudis, Psy.D., MBA

Inception.

The starting point of an institution.

You may be familiar with the phenomenon of a false awakening. This occurs when someone has a vivid and convincing dream about awakening from sleep, while the dreamer in reality continues to sleep. The experience takes on aspects of having a dream within a dream.

A few years prior to the global financial crisis of 2007–2008, this may have been the experience of many North American headquartered large organizations as they positioned themselves to do business in Mainland China. In a fast-growing marketplace, an outsider's perspective may have been to take a business model that worked wonders elsewhere in the world, replicate it, and open up shop. For some, this was a dream with false awakenings.

Canvassing the landscape at the time, one would see local, small businesses jockeying for customers and market share. To an outsider with resources, a simple approach to compete would have been to implement the same strategies which were proven in the United States and other parts of the world.

In a frenzied climate that may have resembled aspects of the old American Wild West, large brands began implementing successful US Strategies in Mainland China that overshadowed their smaller, local competitors. Early on, celebratory launches could be considered successful simply for an organization's resolve to show up. Getting there and building it, with brand visibility and expansion, meant buyers would come.

As fast as mega brands launched (e.g., Wal-Mart, Best Buy, eBay), they were being outwitted by smaller, nimbler, local Chinese brands. The model was ineffective and not well received by local consumers, and not adjusted to the "CHINA WAY" at that time. The dream could become a nightmare as investments made led to closing business in a short time. Naivete about the complexity of the Chinese market was clear.

Position for the Future

For one of the most admired entertainment organizations in the world, this was about the time The Walt Disney Company had decided to move its Chinese Headquarters from Hong Kong to Shanghai. Like many competitors, Disney's

North American global headquarters had identified unrealized potential in a vibrant but still nascently maturing Shanghai.

The move was significant. Prior to this decision, resources were split into thirds and dedicated to serving Hong Kong, Taiwan, and then Mainland China. Changing focus, Mainland China would become the key.

The transformation plan for the consumer products space was simple. Unlock potential incremental growth while not cannibalizing any of the existing consumer products business. The majority of Disney's consumer products and retail efforts at the time yielded 80% of sales from franchises that included Winnie the Pooh and Mickey Mouse merchandise.

If following in other outsiders' footsteps was the plan, an implementation approach would include: creating a headquarters in Shanghai, and simply implementing what was successful around the world without listening to local differences in culture and business acumen.

The leadership team at Disney's consumer products division headquarters took a step back to consider. The Chairman of consumer products was Andy Mooney. He was no stranger to entering a market and seeing it from a different lens. At first, he needed someone on the ground to lead the newly relocated, start-up-like, regional headquarters business and take it to the next level.

Leadership Mindset: Collaboration and Communication

It would be a natural reflex to install a local leader. Mr. Mooney may have been aware of the dream within the dream perspective. He could see potential that went beyond just establishing the business. He may have believed, as a consumer products vision, something could be created that had never existed prior. To a degree, Shanghai might be a new future center of the world. To make that happen, he needed a leader with an open mindset and ability to communicate both at the global, corporate level as well as with the team being developed in Shanghai.

Enter Guenther Hake. Mr. Hake was tapped and became the senior vice president and general manager for Disney's consumer products business in greater China. A German native, Mr. Hake had prior consumer products successes working for Mr. Mooney in Europe, the UK, and Germany.

Mr. Hake entered a world that, while experiencing double-digit growth, was about to be inflicted with the volatile and uncertain impacts of the global financial crisis. At first, he sought to get to know the culture, balancing existing growth amidst intense marketplace contraction and change.

In a short time, Mr. Hake scoped the main existing challenges. These included cultural differences and instability in the workforce as the WAR FOR TALENT was in full force. Leadership consisted mostly of expatriates and resources were split equally between HK, Taiwan, and Mainland China. The business hinged almost entirely on two franchise intellectual properties.

To truly transform, a secret sauce would be required. The recipe for that sauce was to change status quo to continuity. Mr. Hake would quickly embrace a mantra of straightforward communication between the United States and Chinese management teams. He was open about the issues he intended to fix. He consistently led by collaborating and building trust with stakeholders, communicating decisions, and executing on his commitments. This style earned him the nickname, "Mr. Transparency."

No one gets anything done without partners, and for Mr. Transparency, there were a few keys. First, the executive leadership team at Disney Consumer Products, as headed by Mr. Mooney, was stable. Together, as an Executive Leadership Team (ELT), they had been navigating strategy for a decade by this time. The global anchor was secure.

Second, Mr. Hake also had ongoing guidance, local expertise, and everyday access to Stanley Cheung, the Chairman of Disney Greater China. Thirdly, and most importantly, the leadership team on the ground was a beautiful, diverse set of talent from various regions and backgrounds. Lastly, seeing the need to transform the resource allocation regionally, and to address ongoing talent development to win THE TALENT WAR, Mr. Hake worked closely with global human resources and his local HR leader on how to structurally develop the people.

The importance of the partnerships cited must be emphasized. There was an early bet placed on talent. As the global financial crisis blew up, and necessary cost adjustments were executed fast, Greater China was growing operating income by only one percent annually (2008/2009).

While adjusting cost structures and regional allocations, the investment in developing people was significantly increased. This occurred in two ways. First, by determining who were long term keepers and developing them to ensure retention. Second, via talent acquisition. The prior model relied mostly on external, outside of the local area hires. The focus now shifted to younger, less experienced, licensing industry unproven, local, but ambitious professionals. Again, targeting programs to develop this talent included building a working culture together, gaining access to Mr. Hake, and aligning the long-term vision and short-term goals.

Culture Can Be the Main Meal When Driving Change

The bets paid off. Mr. Hake enabled low management turnover, high employee engagement, and satisfaction. Most importantly, a strong learning culture was established. This culture united the team with shared operating principles that included trust, respect, and fun.

There were subtle but significant learnings that accompanied open communications. The most profound were insights into leadership style. Whereas Mr.

Hake took the position of deep listening when working with his organization and licensee partners in the early going, his people told him he needed to adapt to a Chinese way of doing things. In China, though his teams respected him, people told Mr. Hake to stop asking questions and tell them what he thought and what to do. This request for directives was surprising and required Mr. Hake to adjust. For alignment in actions, it made all the difference.

As with any roller coaster ride, in rebuilding the business from the ground up, there were ups and downs. It was important to identify cost savings while building the noted foundation for sustainable growth. All signals pointed to growth potential in Mainland China. This reality reinforced the move to shift resources away from the existing 30/30/30 split with Hong Kong and Taiwan and put all the focus on Mainland China. Again, although there was a risk in making the commitment to the shift, it created alignment and momentum across the team to go above and beyond.

During the financial crisis, this was the only territory in the world with a growing operating income. In the annual employee surveys, the Chinese consumer products business reported the highest engagement scores across the global division. The greatest failure Mr. Hake reported was a personal one, although it was shared across the team. During the first five years of the transformation, there was no time for anything else but that. While his team members made personal choices to travel the road with him, he believes all of those talented people were challenged in managing a balance between work and life.

Leaders may be challenged to identify a single, most important action that ensures successful transformational change. Mr. Hake had no difficulty doing so. He believes a leader must take responsibility for what will happen, and never defer to blaming a third party. Change creates uncertainty, thus clarity in direction, precision in action, and open communication serve to manage through it.

Trust in the Path You Are Taking

In reflecting on his story, the ultimate test of trust also became the driver that put the organization into hyper-growth mode. Known to control its intellectual property, the global and local consumer products leadership team supported Mr. Hake's request to take leadership of a local, up and rising entertainment property called Xi Yang Yang, and to manage their Consumer Products business without controlling ownership. This was thinking far outside a box and the first such move of its kind.

The decision to headquarter the business in Shanghai set up future growth for years to come. The three greatest enablers of the transformation that took place included culture, action, and people. The word "Glocal" became a catchphrase used across the team. It stood for global strategy with local application and implementation. It reinforced everything Mr. Hake embodied in his leadership. The team honored and designed their vision based on the global strategy received from Corporate Headquarters. They sought to execute it, however, based on local norms and requirements.

Mr. Hake's leadership experience was life-changing. He has taken his mission with him. He believes in mutual respect and wants children to enjoy their life in a peaceful world. To do so, his hope is that Chinese and American people will find a way to co-exist. This would create a world where Americans make China a second home, as opposed to a place to which they merely sell products.

Three Things to Know or Do About Transformational Change

1. **Understand cultural differences.** In China, moving across delivery formats from department stores to specialty retail to e-commerce can happen in a brief window of 12–18 months. Businesses unprepared to deliver and move across those formats will be challenged at best.
2. **Act fast.** If speed to action is necessary to compete, then collaborate, decide, communicate the plan, and make it happen. Say what you will do and deliver on it.
3. **People, people, people.** Reward and recognition may be a go-to page in the talent playbook, but hiring great talent, developing, taking care of, and enabling those people to grow, ensures they will stick around during tough times.

Notes

1. www.sundance.ca/integrated-approach-leading-change, [September 10, 2021].
2. Awarded during Element Media and *Pacific Edge* magazine's annual Business Achievement Awards.
3. Susan Robertson, *REAL Leadership: Waken to Wisdom* (New York: The Books Factory, 2019), 87.
4. Susan Robertson, *REAL Culture: 4 Steps To Build Your Competitive Advantage* (New York: BestsellingBook.com, 2022), 78.

Crowdsourcing (Survey) – Build a Bonfire

Our book has already addressed insights on leading transformational change from nearly 50 experienced senior leaders and experts. What else could we need? Well, as musician Joe Strummer said in what he referred to as Strummer's Law, "No input. No output."

So, we gathered great input from 150 additional people who have led transformational changes, been affected by them, or both. Business leaders, individual contributors, CEOs, entrepreneurs, board members, coaches, consultants, HR practitioners, transformation experts, academics, and others had a lot to contribute to the debate on what it takes to lead successful transformational change.

Through our crowdsourcing process, we built a bonfire of ideas and advice in response to the following question, "*What is the single most important action or step a leader or organization can take to ensure successful and lasting transformational change?*"

Our clients and colleagues provided a wealth of diverse input. Despite a wide range of perspectives and experiences, very specific and clear patterns emerged. In this chapter of the book, you will find a brief summary of the following three primary themes, supported by a sampling of representative quotes that provide context and reinforcement:

1. Go First, but Not Alone
2. Define, Align, and Refine the What and Why
3. Energize the Village

Author's Note – The term "Build a Bonfire" is credited with appreciation to my colleague and friend Eva Sage-Gavin (her essay, Leading Change with Constructive Disruption, *may be found in Chapter 3). Eva used this analogy in 2011–2012 as we were working together with Dr. John Boudreau and many others on the CHREATE Project focused on the future of work and HR. The reference symbolized the desire to foster collaboration and sharing of ideas among previously disconnected efforts and leaders – the need to shift from building independent campfires to a more holistic and integrated bonfire. The metaphor applies extremely well in the context of this book's survey inputs.*

DOI: 10.4324/9781003227137-12

Chapter 7

Survey Says . . .

Go First, but Not Alone

Leading transformational change begins, not surprisingly, with leaders. Our survey respondents offered advice that includes changing yourself first, leading by example, walking the talk, modeling the behaviors expected of others, and holding others accountable.

But, action and progress do not fall solely on the shoulders of any one individual leader. Surrounding oneself with a committed team and other key contributors is essential. Successful leaders of transformational change travel in packs, rather than alone. And, remember . . . leadership can come from anyone, anywhere. It is not about a title, level, or pay grade. Leadership is a capability and state of mind. So, ditch the organization chart and focus on influencers and resistors, no matter where they sit in the organization.

Here is a sampling of what our survey respondents had to say about *going first, but not alone*, in leading transformational change:

- ". . . every successful organizational change begins with a change in the leader and the senior executives. The leader must demonstrate in actions and words that she embodies the change. When people believe that the leader has undergone a fundamental change herself, they will embrace and align accordingly."

  – Lance Miyamoto, Principal, Miyamoto Consulting & Retired Senior Vice President of Human Resources, Catalent

- ". . . be as open to their own personal transformation as they expect others and the organization to be."

  – Linda Hoopes, President, Resilience Alliance

- "Lead by example."

  – Paul Marchand, EVP & CHRO, Charter Communications (AKA Spectrum)

DOI: 10.4324/9781003227137-13

- "Role model the new behavior . . . we mimic those we admire and respect."
  - Josephine Panganiban, Global Change Acceleration Practice Leader, MetLife
- "The leader must relentlessly model behaviors representing those changes at the core of transformation and hold others accountable for behavioral modeling."
  - Mark Lipton, Graduate Professor of Management, The New School/ Parsons School of Design
- ". . . encourage your talent to be the best version of themselves every day by being the best version of yourself."
  - Patti Ippoliti, Lecturer and Lead Faculty, Columbia University
- "Hold the entire management team responsible for the transformation . . . leadership sets the example and is accountable."
  - Lindsey Lindemann, Vice President, Human Resources, Primetals Technologies
- "We are all in the middle of a complex world (VUCA) and this generates anxiety. If our leader has the skill to guide us to a brilliant future, we follow."
  - José Ignacio Tobón, Director, José I. Tobón Consultores
- "Ensure leaders tasked with the change are exactly that – leaders."
  - Rebecca Blucher, President, Piper Group, LLC
- "Be surrounded by a diverse leadership team that is aligned and motivated to fully support, drive, and deliver the transformational outcomes."
  - Adriane Brown, Managing Partner, Flying Fish Partners
- "A good leader understands that nothing is ever accomplished on one's own. Great accomplishments usually come with a great team."
  - Tracy Mitchell, Executive Director, Bay Street Theater
- "Be a servant leader who truly understands what it means to serve the multiple stakeholders of the organization, while walking the talk (eat your own dog food)."
  - Heather Banks, CHRO, Shentel (Shenandoah Telecommunications Company)
- "Without trust, it's difficult to create any lasting transformational change."
  - Christy Zajack, CEO, TEB and Chief Growth Officer at the Economic Ecosystem Accelerator

- "Begin within."
  - Teresa Roche, CHRO, City of Fort Collins, Colorado
- "Employees' lives are mostly impacted by their direct manager, so if their direct manager is committed to change, they are much more likely to be committed as well. Conversely, if their manager is not, then good luck."
  - Larry Emond, Managing Director, Global Leadership Advisory, Gallup

Define, Align, and Refine the What and Why

Our survey respondents told us that leading transformational change demands a definition of mission and purpose, alignment of organizational processes and systems to reinforce expected behaviors and actions, as well as constant adjustment and refinement to overcome obstacles and ensure the execution of lasting results. All along the journey, communicate and listen, experiment and do.

Do more and redo. Leading transformational change is a constant and evolving process. Lather. Rinse. Repeat.

Here is a sampling of what our survey respondents had to say about *defining, aligning, and refining the what and why* in leading transformational change:

- "Define Success Upfront! Be very thoughtful and clear on the few critical outcomes/goals you expect to experience a step-change in performance... for example, ensuring a material and lasting change in the client experience (measured by Net Promoter Score), while improving financial results (measured by Total Shareholder Return)."
  - Dermot O'Brien, Chief Transformation Officer, ADP
- "Two words: Mission Clarity. Be crystal clear about what the organization is in business to accomplish; communicate that mission consistently; and show employees how their individual roles, talents, and passion contribute to achieving it."
  - Claire Chandler, SPHR, President & Founder, Talent Boost
- "Provide ringing clarity about the vision behind the change."
  - Curtis Gray, Principal, Gray & Associates LLC and Retired CHRO, BAE Systems
- "Lead people through the change by providing communication of the vision and need for change, the anticipated outcome and value, the steps that we will be taking, how we anticipate the transformation will change

the way people work, what we are going to do to support people during the change, and frequent updates during the transformation process."

- Michelle Prince, Human Capital Consultant/Executive Coach, MPrince Consulting LLC, Former Global Human Resources Executive at Fortune 500 Companies

- "Provide a compelling vision, explain why transformation is necessary and what is in it for the employees, describe a simple pathway to the goal and a vivid visual of what success looks like, and have a little fun along the way."

- Robert Sherwood, HR Advisor

- ". . . align the business need for change to the individual's personal need to change."

- Don Sather, Career Coach, LHH

- "Ensure relentless communication of the vision about what the company will look like to employees and customers."

- Michael McSally, Board Chairman, Employers Holdings

- "Communicate, listen, adjust, communicate, listen, adjust along the way."

- Joe Ketter, EVP Human Resources, SiteOne Landscape Supply

- "Listen and do."

- Jes Valentin, Vice President, Human Capital & Head, Enterprise Solutions, Enspira

- "Co-create a specific, compelling picture of the future that appeals to the people who will create that future, which is more appealing than what people must leave behind."

- Julie Staudenmier, Co-Chair, Executive Board, FRED (Future of Executive Development) Leadership Forum

- ". . . weave the change into the systems, symbols, and behaviors of the organization . . . it must be embedded to endure."

- Jennifer Cmil, EVP, Human Resources, Newmont Mining

- "Lasting transformation comes from changing the operating INFRA-STRUCTURE that shapes how people act day-to-day: operations, organization, governance, reward models, and policies."

- Eric Severson, Chief People & Belonging Officer, Nieman Marcus Group

- "Describe leadership behavior, expectations, and alignment . . . with metrics and consequences. Get on the bus or goodbye. No one has special rights, reasons, or privileges."

  – Liz Iversen, Retired, Chief Quality and Regulatory Officer, Royal Philips

- "Leaders need to remain adaptable . . . re-evaluate their plan, learn from mistakes, and seize opportunities as they arise."

  – Cynthia Maupin, Assistant Professor of Leadership, Binghamton University School of Management

- "Create a clear vision (and expectations) for the future, get the right people involved (and listen to them), lead from the front, align and integrate inside the organization (link to values/purpose and adapt policies, practices, programs), experiment and learn, persevere through challenges and celebrate success, communicate/communicate/communicate."

  – Stephanie McDonald, Senior HR Executive

Energize the Village

Throughout this book, we have asserted that leading transformational change takes a village, and our survey respondents loudly agree! They advised us to create energy and engagement, promote "pull," involve and listen to those affected by change, cultivate a sense of ownership, and focus on the culture needed to enable and sustain lasting transformational change.

While energy comes from positive progress and momentum, it must be accompanied by the courage and willingness to surface and discuss what is not working, in addition to what is working well. A transformational change plan, without passion and purpose, is just a plan that is one dimensional and lifeless. With passion and purpose, transformational change becomes a movement.

Here is a sampling of what our survey respondents had to say about *energizing the village* in leading transformational change:

- "Create a compelling pull by understanding why and how the transformation matters to others. My favorite example is how Disney 'encourages' the lions on the safari adventure ride to sit on the perfect spot for spectators. They don't train the lion, they make the spot where they want the lion to sit cool on hot days and hot on cool days. The lion loves that spot."

  – Greg Pryor, Senior Vice President, People and Performance Evangelist, Workday

- "Bring the organization to a clear sense of purpose that is relevant, credible, inspiring, and actionable."

  – Jane Edison Stevenson, Vice-Chair, Board and CEO Services, Korn Ferry

- "Know your what and why, then follow through with passion and persistence . . . to energize the desired change."

  – Liz Huldin, Chief People Officer, Cirrus Aircraft

- ". . . recognize that adapting individual behavior (to support a change) is a choice . . . create awareness, educate and empower individuals to help them make the right choice and become early adopters."

  – Leah Haines, Principal Consultant, New Reality

- ". . . every leader needs to be . . . curious. Asking questions is the best way to engage people. 'Could you say more?' are the most powerful four words that leaders can ask amidst transformation."

  – Robert "Jake" Jacobs, President, Jake Jacobs Consulting

- "Involve people at all levels and functions to help define and translate what change means for them at an individual, team, functional, and organizational level. Include changes for behavior, policies, structures, business processes, and other key systems."

  – Kim McEachron, Founder and Senior Consultant, DesignGrowthRx, LLC and Retired CHRO, Genomic Health

- ". . . bubble up ideas from the bottom of the pyramid – this brings ownership . . . nurture an ecosystem of ownership."

  – Rohit Bansal, Director, ADP Private Limited

- "ASK, ASK, ASK the people who are leading and impacted by the change for insights, input, and perspectives . . . The more you crowdsource and show genuine care and concern for people, the more they will get behind the change – which will accelerate the process and results."

  – Lisa Jackson, CEO, Corporate Culture Pros

- "Engage the subjects of the change in formulating it, so they develop an intellectual AND emotional attachment to the change."

  – Steve Fitzgerald, CEO, Firestorm Group Ltd, Ex CPO of Bridgewater Associates, and CHRO at Visteon and Vail Resorts

- ". . . have the courage to call out the pain points. Having courageous conversations about change goes a long way in enabling transformation."

- Pallavi Ridout, Founder & CEO, The ELM Advisory Group

- "Get very clear about your organization's real culture and true core values before embarking on significant change. Do an honest assessment of the current state."

  - Joseph Bosch, Principal, HB Consulting and Retired CHRO, DirecTV

- "Put in place a set of 3-5 'Winning Culture Values' after consultation with and support from all stakeholders. Embed the cultural values into basic business processes."

  - Bob Zierk, Retired, Former CHRO of Wernerco

- "All organizations have internal cultures which could be summed up as 'this is the way we do things around here' and are passed down . . . through social example and pressure . . . communicate in word and gesture that 'this is the way we are going to do things around here starting today.'"

  - Ana Daniel, Retired Consultant, McKinsey & Co.

- "Leaders must pay attention to . . . the organization CULTURE (win hearts and minds and understand practices and norms that help or hinder acceptance)."

  - Dr. Orly Maravankin, President, Edge Consulting

- "Don't view it as transformation. View it as renovation instead (see www.culturerenovation.com for more details!)."

  - Kevin Oakes, CEO, i4cp

Part III

Actions

Chapter 8

Don't Do It

Part III of this book is all about summarizing and prioritizing the actions needed to lead transformational change. However, we sometimes benefit from understanding what we *should not* do, before we settle on what we *should* do.

Early in the book, we mentioned that *The Secret Sauce for Leading Transformational Change* would provide insights about why transformational change efforts so often fail. Throughout the book, in various ways, we have shared examples, stories, lessons learned, and actions that address what to do to successfully lead transformational change. The implication is, "do these things and your transformational change will be effective and deliver the intended results."

However, we have also learned – explicitly and implicitly – about what *not* to do. In case it is not yet clear, if you want to effectively lead transformational change, DON'T . . .

1. Do it by yourself
2. Refuse to tell people what needs to be changed, or why
3. Expect people to trust or follow you blindly
4. Make people feel stupid or disloyal if they raise questions or push back
5. Ignore data that conflicts with your preferred view of the internal or external environment
6. Believe that everything will go according to plan, and choose not to adapt
7. Be frustrated or surprised when you fail and have to push the reset button
8. Blame others for your shortcomings or mistakes
9. Look for one magic pill instead of a systemic/holistic set of solutions
10. Confuse doing things differently with improving results (change and transformation are *not* the same)

If you do some, most, or all of the above things, you will likely fail at transformational change!

Now, let us move on to what you *should* do, what we call, "the secret sauce for leading transformational change."

DOI: 10.4324/9781003227137-15

Chapter 9

The Secret Sauce

So, what have we learned in writing – and reading – *The Secret Sauce for Leading Transformational Change*? To answer this question, we should begin by acknowledging and thanking the authors of over 10,000 books that have the words "transformation" or "change" in the title (Source: Amazon.com). There is a lot of really good stuff out there (along with some not-so-good-stuff) on what it takes to lead, manage, master, survive, or learn from change or transformation. One thing that experts all seem to agree on is that change is complicated, difficult, and elusive. Not surprisingly, most contributors to our book agree with this assessment.

There might, however, be some disagreement with other resources about what transformational change is or is not, as well as how to make it stick. In a "typical" book, we likely would have provided a clear definition of transformational change up front, early in the book. But, we chose a different path. We wanted you to read the book first, formulate your own views, and decide whether you agree or disagree with our contributors. Then, share a definition of transformational change so you can decide for yourself whether it resonates with your take. Here is how I define transformational change...

"Transformational change is completely rethinking and repositioning the what, why, how, who, when, and where associated with dramatically improving the effectiveness, happiness, health, and/or survival of someone or something."

Authors often write books to educate and teach the reader. But, we should also be learning from the experience as well. I have learned that I had a lot to learn about transformational change! Here are some ahas that stood out for me as the lead author of this book:

- Leaders are important to transformational change, but leadership is even more important. Everyone can provide leadership of transformational change, whether or not their job title or the organization chart says they are a leader.
- To paraphrase the inventor, Thomas Edison, there is a fine line between vision and hallucination. Having a vision for transformational change

DOI: 10.4324/9781003227137-16

matters, but having an execution plan to get there that everyone understands really makes a big difference.

- People hate change, but they hate failure even more. Transformational change that translates into winning is supported and often enthusiastically embraced as a strategy for survival and success.
- Nothing is impossible for those who do not have to do it. Transformational change is most effective when it is simple and practical, not when it is made more complicated or grandiose than necessary.

After integrating and connecting the dots among nearly 200 contributors to this book, we have curated a broad array of viewpoints. Now that you have had the benefit of reading these wide-ranging insights, we want to focus your attention on the top ten most differentiating ingredients for success. Think of these actions as the formula, *the secret sauce*, for leading transformational change. Each ingredient is briefly summarized to help you capture what matters most for individuals, teams, organizations, and societies going through transformational change. And, as chef Anthony Bourdain used to say, "An ounce of sauce covers a multitude of sins."

Ingredient #1 Start with Truth, Talent, and Timing
1.1   Confront reality
1.2   Surround yourself with people who can make things happen
1.3   Take action faster and more decisively than feels comfortable

Ingredient #2 Cultivate the Spirit of Abundance
2.1   Raise the bar for everyone
2.2   Collaborate to compete and win
2.3   Share what you learn with others

Ingredient #3 Answer from What to What?
3.1   Know where you came from and where you are going
3.2   Clarify what needs to be preserved
3.3   Prioritize what must change

Ingredient #4 Appreciate the Beauty of "And"
4.1   Reconcile competing priorities
4.2   Master paradox
4.3   Recognize that all transformation is change, but not all change is transformational

Ingredient #5 Embrace VUCA (Volatility, Uncertainty, Complexity, Ambiguity)
5.1   See around corners

5.2   Connect the dots
5.3   Enjoy the ride

Ingredient #6 Go First, but Not Alone
6.1   Transform yourself, before changing others
6.2   Lead by example
6.3   Travel in packs

Ingredient #7 Define, Align, and Refine the What and Why
7.1   Set the vision to achieve mission clarity
7.2   Measure success and hold people accountable
7.3   Adjust course along the way

Ingredient #8 Energize the Village
8.1   Create excitement, engagement, and fun
8.2   Cultivate a sense of ownership
8.3   Turn the plan into a movement

Ingredient #9 Love Influencers and Resistors
9.1   Find change leaders at every level
9.2   Treat skeptics like truth-seekers, not as enemies
9.3   Ignore the organization chart

Ingredient #10 Taste-Test the Secret Sauce
10.1 Choose success and results over continuity and tradition
10.2 Take nothing for granted
10.3 Reimagine, reinvent, and reposition almost everything

As you ponder whether leading transformational change is worth the effort, keep in mind a favorite quote from Amazon founder, Jeff Bezos, "Day Two is stasis. Followed by irrelevance. Followed by excruciating, painful decline. Followed by death. And, that is why it is always Day One…"

Make every day "Day One."

Chapter 10

A "Pizzanalogy"

Question: What the f*#k does pizza have to do with leading transformational change? Answer: Everything.

Pizza, like change, can be found almost everywhere and has been around nearly forever, or at least since AD 997, when it was thought to be invented in Gaeta, Italy. These days, approximately 13% of the US population consumes pizza on any given day. As of 2020, pizza industry revenues were $46 billion in the United States alone, and $145 billion worldwide.[1]

Then, how and why would something as ubiquitous (and awesome) as pizza need to be transformed so many times, in so many ways, over so many years? Pizza, like transformational change, is not only subject to continuous revision and the endless quest for perfection, it is defined by it. Pizza is the ideal analogy for, and official food of, leading transformational change. And, do not forget about the secret sauce!

In fact, many of us have discovered that pizza has become a central part of our lives. As actor Bill Murray reminds us, "Unless you are a pizza, the answer is yes, I can live without you."

Just about every product, service, and industry has been reimagined, reinvented, and repositioned to some degree. None more so than pizza, which has encountered an endless array of external forces of change and recurring challenges that have demanded transformational changes in response. Your business and life are likely no different.

Global competition. Regional and local differentiation. Evolving consumer tastes and preferences. Economic uncertainties. Price pressures. Supply chain issues. Health and wellness concerns. Battles between big chain titans like California Pizza Kitchen, Domino's, Papa John's, and Pizza Hut, and the more than 78,000 other large, medium, and mom and pop pizza locations in the United States alone as of 2020.[2] And, the United States is not even the world leader in per capita pizza consumption. That honor, perhaps surprisingly, belongs to Norway.[3]

As a result of these and other trends, pizza is no longer just pizza. Shapes include round, square, rectangle, and oblong. Sizes range across extra-large,

DOI: 10.4324/9781003227137-17

large, medium, small, personal, and slice. Toppings have morphed from old standards such as sausage, pepperoni, meatball, onion, peppers, and mushrooms to now include relative newcomers such a barbeque chicken, broccolini, artichokes, pumpkin, spinach, arugula, and pineapple. Cheeses range from mozzarella, provolone, parmesan, and American, to ricotta, blue, Fontana, and goat. Crusts include white, wheat, gluten free, flatbread, focaccia, French bread, bagel, thin, thick, thicker, pan, deep dish, stuffed, and cauliflower. Cauliflower?

Preparation tools feature the pizza oven, brick oven, wood-fired oven, microwave oven, and toaster oven to cook fresh and frozen varieties. Access options include in-store, take-out, take and bake, and delivery. Secret sauces involve red, white, barbeque, pesto, kabob, and all manner of spices from around the world.

These options are only a small sampling of what is available and evolving in the pizza universe. When it comes to pizza, almost anything goes. And, as pizza goes, so goes the world of transformational change. Pizza is the perfect analogy, the "Pizzanalogy," for leading transformational change because, as we learned from Mike Tyson in Chapter 1, pizza keeps getting punched in the mouth and changing its plans accordingly.

When I was in my teens and early twenties, my friends and I would frequent a place called Dick and Dora's restaurant in Massapequa, New York, to have our favorite, shrimp pizza. Even though the establishment closed nearly four decades ago, I can still smell and taste their shrimp pizza. I smile every time I think about it, in much the same way I smile when I think about my wife, kids, and granddaughter. I loved that pizza like family!

Speaking of family, mine is a pretty good example of how pizza is transforming people and in turn, how people are leading the transformational change of pizza. Two of my sons order their pizza without cheese (not well-received when my youngest son was living in Italy). One of my daughters-in-law is gluten free. My other daughter-in-law (my granddaughter Zoe's mom) is an arugula and pineapple aficionado. I tease her mercilessly as I stick with my meatball pizza, or shrimp pizza when I find it on occasion. It is never as good as Dick and Dora's shrimp pizza, but the search continues.

So, what is the point of this "Pizzanalogy?" Simple. Pizza shows us that the argument for and evidence of the need to lead transformational change is everywhere. Even and especially in those places where longevity and traditions could easily lull us into a false sense of security. Pizza is no longer pizza. People are no longer people. Teams are no longer teams. Organizations are no longer organizations. Societies are no longer societies. Take nothing for granted. Assume everything is up for grabs. We are all works in progress.

The endless pursuit of excellence in all we do represents the beginning, not the end, of leading transformational change. But, what about the secret sauce?

The most important ingredient is knowing that the secret does not remain a secret for very long. We have to push the reset button, mix things up, experiment with new ingredients and recipes and test new flavors and textures. The secret sauce in leading transformational change is us, and our willingness and ability to reimagine, reinvent, and reposition almost everything – especially the secret sauce.

If you need one final dose of inspiration to accompany your transformational change journey, be heartened by this anonymous flash of insight, "Believe in yourself. If cauliflower can become pizza, you can become anything."

Notes

1. www.thoughtco.com/history-of-pizza-1329091, [June 19, 2021].
2. www.statista.com/statistics/377597/number-of-pizza-restaurants-us/, [June 19, 2021].
3. www.puretravel.com/blog/2020/04/06/who-eats-the-most-pizza-in-the-world-the-answer-may-surprise-you/, [June 19, 2021].

Appendix – A Picture Is Worth a Thousand Words

We are in a never-ending quest to make leading transformational change as tangible, practical, and useful as possible. Think of this Appendix as an extra set of tools in your tool kit to help achieve these objectives.

Six of our contributing authors shared their favorite frameworks or models to help you think through or visualize important aspects of transformational change – including cultural, diversity, leadership, operational, individual, team, and organizational dimensions. Each tool is briefly explained, both as to its relevance and its utility.

We encourage you to use these tools as needed to address specific challenges in leading transformational change. As Frenchman and General Napoleon Bonaparte said, "A picture is worth a thousand words."

Managing Fear by Quarantining It

Almost every challenge will bring up some fear. Fear that is not managed will be a barrier to transformational change. The following is a process that will lessen fear's power to block you from accomplishing your most important goals.

1. Recognize that you are having some fear and decide to **acknowledge** and address it.
2. Schedule a time to **meet** with that fearful part of you.
3. Give that part of you a **name** other than your own. For example: Fearful Frank or Fearful Fran. By doing this, you are acknowledging that it is a part of you that is fearful and not all of you. This lessens the fear.
4. Ask that fearful part of you to share everything he/she is experiencing. Do not speak other than to ask, "What else are you afraid of?" You are to **listen** and write down everything said. This is letting your subconscious know that you are taking this seriously. Eventually fear will run out of steam.
5. Set up a meeting for the next day and **repeat** the process. Fear will have less and less to say.

6. Fear will want to intrude on your life beyond this meeting. You must **remind** it that there is a time to meet and that you will not listen to fear at any other time.

Figure A-1 A circular cycle diagram representing the process of Quarantining Fear (Harris/Ziskin, 2021).

Quarantining Fear, with permission from Marisa Harris and Ian Ziskin (2021).

The Adaptive Cycle of Change

Organizations evolve through cycles of change and disruption, with each cycle having four stages. By building both individual and organizational capability at each stage of the cycle, transformational change leaders create conditions for thriving in dynamic and complex environments.

Focusing on the adaptive cycle enables leaders to help their organizations:

- Build a resilient foundation for today and tomorrow
- Continuously adapt to promote agility, innovation, and relevance
- Release what no longer serves a purpose, to unleash potential for reinvention

A CONTINUOUS CYCLE OF EVOLUTION:
Four stages of Growth and Development

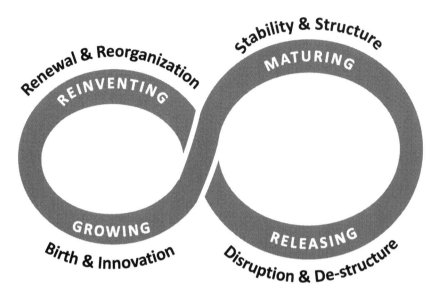

Figure A-2 A Continuous Cycle of Evolution (Heffelfinger/Parker, 2021).

The adaptive cycle equips leaders to navigate and perform through change and disruption so their organizations can thrive. They take these steps:

- **Diagnose** themselves (attitudes, behaviors, habits) and their organizations (history, patterns, culture).
- **Value diversity and engage diverse views** to create a fuller picture of the dynamic nature of their organizations and their environments.
- **Take strategic action**, *i.e.*, knowing what distinctive or core capabilities to build on and what to release (processes, products, mindsets) to generate new/enhanced/competitive business models and solutions.

For more information see Lori Heffelfinger and Sally Breyley Parker's essay, *Transformation Through Adaptive Leadership*, in Chapter 5 of this book.

The Adaptive Cycle of Change, with permission from Lori Heffelfinger and Sally Breyley Parker (2021).

Individual Tool: Breaking Cultural Patterns

As stated in the *Sustainable Diversity, Equity, and Inclusion (DEI): Transformational Change at the Individual, Team, and Organizational Levels* essay in Chapter 5 of this book, "Most people believe a company culture is beyond their ability to influence. The reality is that . . . one person can indeed make a difference." One of the ways they can do this is by breaking unproductive behavioral patterns that occur in day-to-day interactions.

The approach below helps individuals to analyze, deconstruct, and reconstruct dynamics where they themselves participate. By identifying and recognizing when the "triggers" kick off undesirable exchanges, they can change their own responses and therefore compel others to do the same. Those new behavioral patterns will evolve into new cultural patterns when they are repeatedly practiced over time.

BREAKING CULTURAL PATTERNS

OBSERVE   ANALYZE   RESET

- Situation
- Trigger
- Behavior or Pattern
- Response(s)
- Outcome

- Espoused Value
- Actual Value
- Meaning of Any Gap

- Desired Value
- Plan
- Recognize
- New Behavioral Pattern
- New Response(s)
- New Outcome(s)

Breaking Cultural Patterns, with permission from Karen Jaw-Madson (2021).

Team Tool: Team Charter Template

When colleagues collaborate on creating their team charter, they are negotiating an agreement on how they expect to interact: their team culture. The process itself engages and enrolls members as they thoughtfully align and commit to one another. By answering the prompt questions below, a team will be able to organize and refine content using the questions in the boxes below.

The charter serves as a reference guideline and a way of measuring their progress as a team once it is implemented. Be reminded that a tool is only as good as its usefulness. A team must have the discipline to stick to this social contract *every day* in order to get the intended results.

TEAM CHARTER TEMPLATE

- *What's important to us?*
- *How do we engage each other and commit?*
- *How can we establish psychological safety and trust?*
- *What norms do we want to emphasize?*
- *How will we role model diversity, equity, and inclusion?*
- *How will we manage conflict?*
- *How will we cultivate connection?*

Table A-1 Team Charter Template (Jaw-Madson, 2018).

Our Purpose: Why does this team exist? What is its primary purpose?	
Our Process: What process(es) will be developed, implemented, or used by this team? What will guide the progression of activities toward the defined outcome?	
Our Norms: • Define <u>behaviors</u> characteristic of this team, its culture, and how it will work together (minimum 5–7, no more than 10–12)	**Operating Principles:** • What principles explain and guide the norms? (minimum 5–7, no more than 10–12)

Team Charter Template, with permission from Karen Jaw-Madson (2018).

Organizational Tool: Design of Work Experience (DOWE) Framework

Design of Work Experience (DOWE) is a strengths-based, co-creation framework that provides the much-needed step-by-step for designing, implementing, and sustaining organizational culture, and employee experiences that are customized to an organization's unique context. The DOWE process comprises four main components: DESIGN and CHANGE processes enabled by the use and development of CAPABILITY and ENGAGEMENT throughout.

There are five phases, each organized as a progressive series of learning loops with specific activities:

- **UNDERSTAND:** determines a full baseline of the current state through a Culture Study
- **CREATE & LEARN:** combines learning and creative design processes to uncover new possibilities
- **DECIDE:** iterates toward a selection of solutions and the creation of the Strategy & Design Blueprint
- **PLAN:** prepares the organization for the implementation of the Blueprint with Roadmap & Action Plans
- **IMPLEMENT:** manages change and transformation toward the intentionally designed future state

DOWE provides an in-depth understanding of the current state, a strategy and design for the future state, and a roadmap with action plans for how to get there.

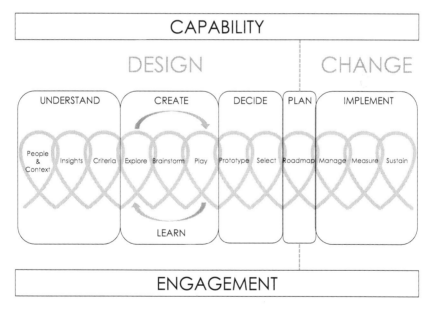

Figure A-3 Design of Work Experience (Jaw-Madson, 2018).

Design of Work Experience – Detailed View, with permission from Karen Jaw-Madson (2018).

Theoretical Model of Inclusive Leadership

This model (see Figure A-4) explores inclusiveness as it relates to leadership by demonstrating the relationship between the two. Individual differences (pro-diversity beliefs, humility, cognitive complexity) factor into inclusive leadership behaviors that contribute to team* members' perceptions of inclusion. This process results in team identification and empowerment. In turn, behavioral outcomes include increased creativity, stronger job performance, and reduced turnover.

Leading transformational change is enhanced by fostering pro-diversity beliefs and showing humility. This model assumes we can teach leaders the value of cognitive complexity on teams. To determine if you can improve on perceptions of inclusion and behavioral outcomes, focus on developing the inclusive leadership skills listed in the model shown here. Listen to team member feedback about their experience on their teams, and whether they positively identify with their team and/or experience psychological empowerment. You can also collect data on job performance and turnover to help determine success.[1]

team = work group

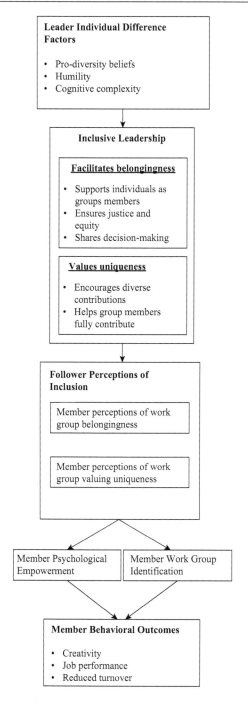

Figure A-4 Theoretical Model of Inclusive Leadership (Randel, 2018).

Leading Change

This simple Leading Change framework (see Table A-2) is structured to acknowledge a few truths about leading transformational change. First, change is complicated, but the way you lead it does not need to be. Second, people are complicated, but the way you lead them does not need to be. Third, I have sometimes made leading change more complicated than it needed to be, and have learned that it is okay to push the reset button.

The framework addresses the single most important question in leading transformational change, "From what to what?" This question ensures we do not throw the baby out with the bath water by making sure we first understand where we are coming from before locking in on where we are going to.

"For what reasons?" is critical to understanding our priorities and focus. Are we trying to improve operating margins, grow revenue, become more globally competitive, be more customer-centric, reduce bureaucracy, be more collaborative, drive innovation, become a better place to work, or what?

"What is the risk of unintended consequences?" is my way of asking whether we know how changing one aspect of the organization will affect other dynamics.

"What role do key leaders play?" is really a two-part question. First, who are the key leaders (and influencers) we must engage in the process? Second, what do we want them to do?

Table A-2 Leading Change Framework (Ziskin, 2015)

1. From what to what?	2. For what reasons?
3. What is the risk of unintended consequences?	4. What role do key leaders play?
5. What are the likely resistance points, and how do we overcome them?	6. How do we know whether we are going too far, or too fast?

Leading Change Framework, with permission from Ian Ziskin (2015).

"What are the likely resistance points, and how do we overcome them?" is the flip side of the coin from understanding influencers. Resistance points can be people, organizations, sacred cows, or other issues that we can assume will be difficult to address and win over.

"How do we know if we are going too far, or too fast?" is often the toughest question to answer. But, one thing is certain: there is very little correlation between moving too far or too fast, and whether people like the change being implemented (if they have made up their minds to oppose it). So, put your energy into doing it right by addressing all the above questions first, and then adjust the speed and intensity as you go.[2]

Notes

1. Amy Randel, Benjamin Galvin, Lynn Shore, Karen Holcombe Ehrhart, Beth Chung, Michelle Dean, and Uma Kedharnath, "Inclusive Leadership: Realizing Positive Outcomes Through Belongingness and Being Valued for Uniqueness," *Human Resource Management Review* 28, no. 2 (June 2018): 190–203.
2. Ian Ziskin, *THREE: The HR Emerging Executive* (New York: Wiley, 2015), 56–61.

Acknowledgments

This book is a collective team effort from start to finish. I want to begin by thanking our members of the Consortium for Change (C4C) (https://businessinsitegroup.com/consortium-for-change/), who serve as a constant source of collaboration and inspiration for me and one another. In particular, I would like to thank Lacey Leone McLaughlin, my C4C co-founder.

While this book has been a highly collaborative project, some people have stepped up in big ways to take on leadership roles. We used a number of teams to help pull the book together. Special thanks to the Essays team leaders (Sophia Kristjansson and Adrienne Shoch), Interviews team leaders (Kim McEachron and David Yudis), Marketing team leaders (Kelly Bean and Tracy Tyler), Tools team leaders (Steve Fitzgerald and Lori Heffelfinger), Writing and Editing team leaders (Jennifer Green and Jennifer McEwen), and Publishing team leaders (Maria Forbes and Cheryl Perkins). You were awesome, as were the authors who contributed interviews and essays for this book, cited throughout, and the team members who helped in ways too numerous to mention.

The Secret Sauce for Leading Transformational Change required hands-on program management all the way through to keep dozens of contributing authors on track and on time. Gina Sorrells handled it all with style, grace, and incredible professionalism. Thank you for your sense of humor and epic attention to detail, I could not have written the book without you. Likewise, my executive assistant, Heather Coleman-Otuyelu, was a great partner in keeping the rest of our business running smoothly while the book often consumed my attention. I appreciate your constant support.

The team at Routledge, Taylor & Francis Group, including Editor Meredith Norwich, Editorial Assistant Chloe Herbert, Production Editorial Manager Stacey Carter, Deputy Production Editorial Manager Helen Evans, Project Manager Aruna Rajendran, and Production Editor Naomi Holliman provided expert guidance and encouragement throughout the book conception, writing, editing, marketing, and publishing processes. THANK YOU!

Finally, my family is my reminder of why I do what I do, and they provide me the flexibility, support, understanding, and love required to do it. Many thanks to my wife (Susan), sons (Tyler, Eric, and Matt), daughters-in-law (Amy and Kajsa), granddaughter (Zoe), new granddaughter on the way, mom (Marilyn), and brother (Adam). You are my village, and I love you all.

Contributor Biographies

Kelly Bean, *Principal of Heron Strategy Partners (Heron), is a prominent leadership and executive development expert. She has been a professor, dean, and CEO of UCLA Anderson, Emory Goizueta, WashU Olin, WashU at Brookings, and UVA Darden. Heron is a collaborative of learning leaders that provide learning, leadership, and advisory services to organizations and individuals.*

Dr. John Boudreau *is a globally recognized thought-leader, award-winning researcher, Professor Emeritus at the University of Southern California's Marshall School of Business, and a Senior Research Scientist at its Center for Effective Organizations,* **and Jonathan Donner** *advises organizations about the future of leadership and organizational capability; he was the Vice President of Global Learning and Capability Development at Unilever from 2009 to 2016 and in more recent assignments with the UN World Food Programme and Amazon.*

Dr. Beth Banks Cohn, *President of ADRA Change Architects, is an accomplished Organizational Consultant, Senior Executive Coach, Entrepreneur, and Thought Leader with more than 25 years of success in helping individuals and organizations use change as a strategic advantage.*

Rebecca Feder, *Principal Consultant of Princeton HR Insight LLC, is a seasoned HR executive who has been consistently recognized for innovative solutions that drive alignment and deliver results. She has coached hundreds of executives and teams to understand how motivation and different management styles can positively impact performance to accelerate effectiveness. Her approach focuses on identifying areas of impact, then designing and delivering programs that link HR actions to business strategy to ensure that goals are achieved, initiatives are sustained, and the company is ready to meet future demands.*

Steve Fitzgerald *is the CEO of the Firestorm Group Ltd, where he consults on the topic of human capital strategy and serves on various Boards. His executive career spanned 30+ years, in which he held the Chief HR/Talent Officer position at Bridgewater Associates, Visteon, Vail Resorts, and Fairlane Credit.*

Maria Forbes, *Managing Director, Hitch UP Inc., focuses on strategic alignment among leadership teams and how they engage colleagues at all levels in developing strategy and business change initiatives. She has a proven record of achievements and a long career in strategic and global organization change, addressing a broad range of needs to enable successful execution of business strategy, including leader alignment, business transformation, and employee engagement in organizations across multiple industries and geographies.*

Barbara Frankel, *CEO of Coaching Initiatives LLC, partners with C-level executives and their teams to align leadership and transform the culture to be fully engaged and thrive. Prior to leading her own business for 15+ years, Barbara worked in Human Resources for JPMorgan Chase and American Express.*

Marisa Harris, *Founder of Transformational Solutions, is an accomplished coach, teacher, and consultant, who empowers leaders with a life-threatening cancer to recognize and apply the universal principles of success to their health challenges. Her application of leadership principles to her own life-threatening diagnosis of stage 4 pancreatic cancer in 1998, has been featured in publications, on media, and most recently in the book* FULFILLED! Critical Choices: Work, Home, Life, *by William A. Schiemann.*

Lori Heffelfinger *is the Founding Partner of The Heffelfinger Company Inc., a consultancy instrumental in helping leaders, teams, and organizations get to the heart of issues to positively impact relationships, productivity, and the bottom line. Lori led Organization Development and HR functions at Honeywell and Raytheon, helping them transform leaders, their functions, and businesses,* **and Sally Brey-ley Parker** *of Time Zero Enterprises focuses on unleashing the life force of leaders, teams, and organizations through living systems strategy, design, and development. Sally speaks and teaches globally on living systems strategy and design, and has led transformation efforts in all sectors to enhance sustainability, performance, culture, and well-being.*

Robert "Jake" Jacobs *is President of Jake Jacobs Consulting, a global consulting firm focused on helping clients achieve faster, easier, better results than they ever imagined possible,* **and Susan Schmitt Winchester** *is the CHRO for Applied Materials and a leading voice for teaching people how to use the workplace as a laboratory for emotional healing from dysfunctional pasts, where they can build the future they deserve.*

Karen Jaw-Madson *is principal of Co.-Design of Work Experience, author of* Culture Your Culture: Innovating Experiences @ Work *(Emerald Group Publishing, 2018), founder of Future of Work platform A New HR, an executive coach, and instructor at Stanford University's Continuing Studies Program. She empowers organizations through coaching and developing leadership, enabling them to leverage culture, diversity, and employee experience, optimizing their talent, and driving change management and transformation.*

Sophia Kristjansson *works with leaders to maximize organizational potential. She is the principal of Lexicon Lens, a boutique consulting firm in DEI, change management, and people development. She is also a member of the faculty at the University of Denver in organizational leadership, strategic human resource practices, and diversity, equity, and inclusion best practices.*

Heather Laychak *is Vice President and Chief People Officer for The Aerospace Corporation. She has over 20 years of experience in Human Resources in both for-profit and nonprofit companies across multiple industries including aerospace and defense, academia, retail, entertainment, and healthcare. Heather was a founding member of the American Red Cross Auxiliary Board in Chicago, IL. She currently serves as a board member for ANSER and the National Kidney Foundation, Southern California Chapter, and is a Salzburg Global Seminar Fellow.*

Dr. Orly Maravankin, *President of Edge Consulting Inc., is a Senior Executive Coach, Business Executive, and Thought Leader. She helps leaders build skills to thrive in today's complex environment, cultivate high-performance cultures, and lead with clarity and purpose.*

Alan May *is the Executive Vice President and Chief People Officer for Hewlett Packard Enterprise. Alan's strategic leadership has been instrumental in aligning culture and organizational structure to achieve the company's bold goals for transformation and growth. Prior to HPE, he held several senior HR leadership roles at The Boeing Company, Cerberus Capital Management, and PepsiCo.*

Jennifer E. McEwen, Ph.D., *Co-Founder of LAITHOS | The Leadership Impact Company, has a track record of over 20 years of leading large-scale organizational transformation. As an experienced coach and proven executive in Fortune 100 companies, she works with C-level executives and teams to align leadership, culture, and strategy to improve organizational health and relationships.*

Lacey Leone McLaughlin, *Principal and Executive Coach at LLM Consulting Group, brings 20 years of experience to her executive coaching and talent management consulting practice. Lacey has worked with clients across all industries and sizes including aerospace, automotive, entertainment, media, professional services, retail, and technology, ranging from entrepreneurial-led start-ups to Global/Fortune 100 companies.*

Linda Naiman *helps executives and their teams develop creativity, innovation, and leadership capabilities through coaching, training, and consulting. She brings a multi-disciplinary perspective to learning and development through arts-based learning and design thinking. Clients include Cisco Systems, Dell, Intel, BASF, and the UN. Linda is founder of Creativity at Work, and co-author of* Orchestrating Collaboration at Work: Using Music, Improv, Storytelling, and Other Arts to Improve Teamwork.

Dermot O'Brien *is the recently retired Chief Transformation Officer at ADP and the prior CHRO at ADP and TIAA. With close to 20 years of reporting to*

CEOs and over 30 years of leading global HR teams, Dermot has deep operating business experience and possesses a special ability to embrace and engage the Human Balance Sheet through growth and change. A native of Dublin, Ireland, he attended University in New York, and has lived and worked in Hong Kong, Japan, and the United States.

Cheryl Perkins, *CEO and Founder of Innovationedge, LLC, is a thought leader with over 35 years of experience in innovation, and as a business strategy expert, prominent keynote speaker, published author, and creative catalyst in brand-building initiatives.*

Patrick R. Powaser, Ph.D. *is Founder and President of Ho'ohana Coaching & Consulting. He provides executive coaching and leadership consulting services to inspire his clients to transform their organizations and achieve greater results. Prior to founding his consulting practice, Pat spent 25 years inside Fortune 500 corporations (Bank of America, Frito-Lay, The Limited, Occidental Petroleum). He is based in Kaua'i, Hawai'i, with clients across the islands, the US mainland, and international locations.*

Susan Robertson *is Co-Founder and CEO, Linceis Conscious Business. She is an executive coach, culture transformation specialist, and author of* REAL Leadership: Waken to Wisdom, and REAL Culture: 4 Steps to Build Your Cultural Competitive Advantage.

Linda Rogers *is the Chief People and Places Officer at Dolby Laboratories. She is a forward-thinking strategist who brings together expert creators to innovate and discover in agile work environments as global citizens. Throughout her 20+ year career, she has acted as the steward of companies' global talent ecosystems and curated the conditions for people to do their best work and drive business growth,* **and Tessa Finlev** *is Dolby Laboratories' first ever Foresight Strategist. Her primary focus is on designing shared processes for understanding emerging futures and connecting the dots to strategy, innovation, and company culture. In her decade-plus in the foresight field, Tessa has traveled the world teaching, presenting, and researching possible futures for a wide range of audiences.*

Eva Sage-Gavin *is a distinguished C-Suite thought leader and former CHRO, with more than three decades of experience in Fortune 500 global consumer and technology corporations. She is a Board Director and most recently served as senior managing director for Accenture's global talent & organization consulting practice.*

Deb Seidman *is Founder and President of Green Silk Associates, LLC, a consulting firm specializing in organization effectiveness. Throughout a 30+ year career, as a corporate HR practitioner and as an external consultant, she has gained extensive experience with change management, organization design, and HR talent practices.*

Adrienne Shoch *is a Holistic Innovationist and Founder of 5 to 1 Consulting, LLC. She is a thought leader, leadership coach, trainer, and former Director of Thales University North America, guiding clients to navigate how the brain, body, and communication influence behavior, performance, and connection.*

Padma Thiruvengadam *has a proven track record of improving organizational performance by building multi-dimensional capabilities for companies across several industries. She leads through change, transformation, influence, and impact to establish and exceed breakthrough corporate and people objectives. Padma has been the CHRO for Takeda Pharmaceuticals, CPO for Lego, and CHRO for Integra Lifesciences.*

David Yudis, Psy.D., MBA *is President and Founder of Potential Selves Inc., a leadership development corporation that delivers business growth through the transformation of talent. Providing executive coaching and team effectiveness services, he is a member of and has been published as part of Forbes Coaches Council and has appeared on ABC, CBS, Fox, and NBC networks as a speaker on how organizations achieve success.*

About the Lead Author

Ian Ziskin, President, EXec EXcel Group LLC, has 40 years of experience as a business leader, board advisor and member, coach, consultant, entrepreneur, teacher, speaker, and author. He is the Co-Founder and Partner of Business inSITE Group (BiG), Co-Founder of the Consortium for Change (C4C), and Co-Founder of the CHREATE Project. His global leadership experience includes Chief Human Resources Officer and/or other senior leadership roles with three Fortune 100 companies – Northrop Grumman, Qwest Communications, and TRW.

Ian has served as a board director, advisory board member, and senior advisor for multiple companies, professional service firms, associations, universities, and non-profits. He has a Master of Industrial and Labor Relations degree from Cornell University and is a magna cum laude graduate of Binghamton University with a Bachelor of Science degree in Management. In 1988, *Human Resource Executive* magazine named Ian one of 12 "Up and Comers in HR." In 2007, he was elected a Fellow of the National Academy of Human Resources, considered the highest honor in the HR profession.

In addition to his role as the lead author of this book, *The Secret Sauce for Leading Transformational Change* (2022), Ian has written or co-edited three other books including *Black Holes and White Spaces: Reimagining the Future of Work and HR with the CHREATE Project* (2018), *THREE: The Human Resources Emerging Executive* (2015), and *WillBe: 13 Reasons WillBe's Are Luckier than WannaBe's* (2011). He is a contributing author to *The End of Jobs* by Jeff Wald (2020), *The SAGE Handbook of Human Resource Management* edited by Adrian Wilkinson, et. al. (2019), *The Rise of HR: Wisdom From 73 Thought Leaders* edited by Dave Ulrich, et.al. (2015), and *The Chief HR Officer: Defining the New Role of Human Resource Leaders,* edited by Pat Wright, et. al. (2011). Ian has written dozens of articles, blogs, and book chapters on the future of work, HR, leadership, coaching, and HR's role with the board of directors.

Index

Note: Page numbers in *italics* indicate a figure and page numbers in **bold** indicate a table on the corresponding page.

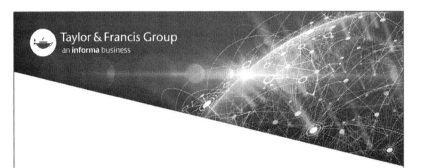